William Lowth

Directions for the Profitable Reading of the Holy Scriptures

William Lowth

Directions for the Profitable Reading of the Holy Scriptures

ISBN/EAN: 9783337779900

Printed in Europe, USA, Canada, Australia, Japan

Cover: Foto ©Lupo / pixelio.de

More available books at **www.hansebooks.com**

DIRECTIONS
FOR THE
Profitable Reading
OF THE
HOLY SCRIPTURES.

TOGETHER

With some OBSERVATIONS for the Confirming their Divine Authority, and Illustrating the Difficulties thereof.

By WILLIAM LOWTH, B. D.
Prebendary of WINCHESTER.

The FIFTH EDITION.

LONDON:

Printed for JOHN HINTON, at the King's-Arms, in Pater-noster Row, near Warwick-lane.
MDCCLXIX.

THE
PREFACE.

FTER so many excellent commentaries and treatises upon the Holy Scriptures, it may seem needless to publish any thing further upon this argument, since it may be presumed that nothing hath escaped the search of so many learned and inquisitive persons, or can be pertinently added upon so common a subject.

I might, by way of apology for the following treatise, truly affirm that some particulars are handled in it, which have not been much insisted on by other writers: Some of the difficulties herein considered having been started, or at least revived, but of late years. But I rather chuse to say, that I cannot think discourses of this kind to be impertinent, as long as so many men of corrupt minds let loose both their tongues and pens against the holy Writings. These all Christians look upon as the oracles of God, and the sacred *Depositum* of divine truth: And whoever retains a due reverence for them, and makes them his study and meditation, will *continue grounded and settled in the faith, and not be moved from the hope of the Gospel* by the little cavils and exceptions of *Sceptics* and *Infidels*, which we may be bold to say proceed from their not knowing the Scriptures, and scorning to use the means whereby they might be better informed.

The *seat of the scorners* is now-a-days looked upon as the only *infallible chair*, and that temper which *Solomon* [a] so frequently brands with the

---

[a] Prov. iii. 34. xiii. 1. xiv. 6. xxix. 8.

worst of characters, as the most incapable of instruction, the most pernicious to him that hath it, and the most dangerous to the public, is thought by many amongst us to be the surest indication of wit and parts. But *whether such persons will hear, or whether they will forbear*, it is certainly the duty of those who are appointed to be *watchmen over the house of* Israel *to warn men to take heed, lest there be in any of them an evil heart of unbelief in departing from the living God*, and despising his holy word, by which they must expect to be judged at the last day. It becomes those *who are set for the defence and confirmation of the Gospel*, to stand in the breach, and endeavour in their several stations, to give a check to the *overflowings of ungodliness*, which threaten to break down all our banks, and whose principles, if they are pursued to their just consequences, cancel the authority of all laws both divine and human, and set men loose from the obligations of them: Licentiousness in opinion always making way for licentiousness in practice, which is the true reason why it finds so many abettors amongst us at this day. Upon which account it is the earnest wish and prayer of many good men, that God would put it into the heart of those who are in authority, to take care that the *Toleration be confined within the bounds which the law hath prescribed to it*; for it is great pity that *liberty of conscience* should become a shelter for *men of no conscience*, to vent such doctrines as are not only destructive of all revealed religion, but even of civil society itself.

It were well if the *teachers* of the *separate congregations* (I mean as many of them as have any regard for a rule of faith or discipline) would shew their zeal upon this occasion, in standing up for the maintenance of those common truths, which all that deserve the name of Christians,

Chriſtians, agree in. It would be great weakneſs in them to take the *author of the rights of the Chriſtian Church*, and men of his ſtamp for their friends, becauſe they diſcover a particular Spite and Hatred to the *Eſtabliſhed Church*: That indeed is the principal Object of Envy, (and we hope it always will be ſo to Men of ill Deſigns) and they are encouraged in their Attempts againſt it, becauſe they hope to find their own account in the unſettling of their foundations: But he muſt be blind that does not ſee, that the ſame arguments which are levelled againſt the preſent eſtabliſhment, may be eaſily applied to other conſtitutions, ſome of which extend their claim to a *jus divinum* farther than the *Church of England* does.

The ſeveral parties that divide us, ſeem to agree in nothing ſo much as in expreſſing a great vehemence againſt *Popery:* Therefore it will not be amiſs briefly to conſider what advantages this licentiousness in opinion, so much in vogue, affords to that very cause, which it declaims against with so much fierceness.

First of all, nothing gives so plausible a colour to the *Popish* boasts of *unity* and *infallibility*, as to see men that pretend so much zeal against it, fall off from the common principles of Christianity, and discard all certainty in matters of religion.

In the next place, *superstition* and *profaneness* are not so far asunder as some may imagine: One extreme doth usually produce another; and when men have for some time bewildered themselves in the *maze* of *scepticism* and *infidelity*, and can find nothing whereon to fix, they will be ready to hearken to the *Popish* pleas for the *infallibility* of the *Church*, or to any thing else that may put a stop to their endless wanderings, and give rest to their weary souls.

Add to this, in the third place, that

that hearty *zeal* for religion, though it proceed upon false principles, will in the end get the better of a *lukewarm* and indifferent temper, which not only makes people suspect that the cause which is so coldly maintained wants truth to support it, but likewise that the abettors of it do not believe themselves.

To recover the spirit of piety, which is so visibly decayed, and almost extinguished amongst us, I cannot but earnestly recommend to all that are sincere lovers of truth, the careful reading of the holy Scriptures, which will afford to all that seriously peruse them, so many *internal arguments* of their divine authority, as cannot be withstood by an ingenuous mind, namely, such as are taken from their general scope and design, and the harmony of the several parts compared with each other; which proofs have this peculiar advantage, that they may be discerned by an ordinary judgment without the help of human learning. It is the principal design of the following Papers, to consider the force of those arguments which arise from the very frame and contexture of the holy Writings. And I heartily pray to God, that the several treatises, which have of late been written upon this and such like subjects, the publishing whereof is so necessary in this age, may, by his blessing, become in some measure useful for the convincing gainsayers, and confirming well-disposed persons in their holy faith.

A
SYNOPSIS
OR
ABRIDGEMENT
OF THE
HOLY SCRIPTURES,

Which teach what Man is to believe concerning GOD, and what Duty GOD requires of Man.

THE word SCRIPTURE signifies *Writing*, and generally stands for the sacred Books of the Old and New Testament written by holy Men as they were inspired, instructed and enabled by the Holy Ghost. They are called the Scriptures by by way of eminency and diftinction, becaufe they far excel all other writings. 2 Tim. iii. 16. "All fcripture is given by infpiration of God, and is profitable for doctrine," to declare and confirm the truth; "for reproof," to convince of fin and confute errors; "for correction," to reform the life; "and for inftruction in righteoufnefs;" that is, to teach us to make a farther progrefs in the way to holinefs and happinefs in heaven; or to inftruct in the true Righteoufnefs of Jefus Chrift, in which we may appear with comfort before God.

The Scriptures are often called, The Bible, that is, The Book, by way of eminency, as being the beft book in the world, and far excelling all other books: For the Scriptures are a revelation from God, and contain his whole will neceffary to be known for our falvation: And they will be in the higheft efteem, and be read and ftudied by all the true members of the church of God, whofe faith, hope and comfort are taken from thefe divine Oracles. No book but this brings fuch glory to God, or hath fuch an efficacy in converting the foul, Pfal. xix. 7.

The holy scripture is divided into two books, which are commonly called, The Old and New Testament, or The Old and New Covenant: The Old Testament was the old dispensation of the Covenant of grace, by types and sacrifices which represented the coming of the Messiah, who was the promised seed of the woman, and afterwards foretold to be of the family of Abraham, and of the tribe of Judah, and of the seed of David.

The New Testament, or the Gospel, is the new dispensation of the Covenant of Grace, which fully shews the promised Messiah to be come, and to have published his gospel, to have died, and to have risen again, and to have ascended up into heaven to plead that his atonement may be accepted as a propitiation for all true believers.

There is no history in the world so ancient as the Bible, nor is there any that gives so early an account of things. The Old Testament begins at the creation of the world, and acquaints us that Adam and Eve were the first man and woman God made, and that he created them both
in

in his own likeness, in a holy and happy state, which is called The state of innocence. It informs us of their sin against God in eating the forbidden fruit, and of their being driven out of paradise, and of the miserable state that sin brought man into, he having broke covenant with God, and being exposed to that dreadful threatning, "In the day thou eatest thereof "thou shalt surely die."

The scripture informs us, that after the fall or sin of Adam God was pleased to give him a gracious promise of a Messiah or Redeemer, " That the seed of the wo-" man should bruise the head of the serpent," that is, that Jesus Christ who was to assume the human nature in the fulness of time should destroy the power and wicked works of the devil.

The religion of man after the fall was all the duties of the light of nature, which were required before : And besides these he was now called to repentance, faith or trust in the mercy of God, and expectation of the promised Saviour, and offering of sacrifices. This is called the Adamitical dispensation, and it reached to Noah's

Of the HOLY SCRIPTURES. 15
Noah's flood, which was about 1656 years after the creation of the world.

The scripture tells us that mankind had provoked God by their sins, which were exceeding great, and that the world was destroyed by a flood for their multiplied iniquities. Noah was saved in an ark or great ship or vessel, which God taught him to build, and all his family were with him, and some living creatures of every kind.

The religion of Noah was the same with that of Adam after his fall, with some few additions. The offering of sacrifices was to be continued. Flesh was given to man for food, as herbs were before. Blood was forbidden to be eaten, the blood of man was expresly forbid to be shed, and murder was to be punished with death, Gen. ix. 2, 3, 4, 5, 6. And this was the Noachical dispensation of the covenant of grace.

After the flood mankind did not freely divide themselves into several nations; but, being all of one language, they built a chief city with a tower, that all men might be joined in one nation or kingdom.

dom. But God scattered them abroad into different nations, by making them speak different languages, and then they ceased to build their tower, which was called Babel or Confusion. It is supposed that the true religion was chiefly preserved in the family of Shem, for God is called " the Lord God of Shem," Gen. ix. 26.

The most religious and most famous man of Shem's posterity in these early ages was Abraham the son of Terah, of the posterity of Eber: He left his own native country to go wheresoever God pleased: He came first from Chaldea, and then to Haran, and by the command of God went to dwell among strangers in the land of Canaan.

Sodom became very wicked, and it was destroyed by fire and brimstone from heaven together with Gomorrah and other cities, because of the abominable wickedness of their inhabitants. Abraham pleaded with God to spare Sodom, and he would have done it, had there been ten righteous men in all the city. Lot was grieved for the wicked conversation of Sodom, and he and his two daughters were saved:

Of the HOLY SCRIPTURES. 17

saved: But his wife looking back and hankering after Sodom, was struck dead immediately, and she stood like a pillar of salt.

Abraham had two sons, Ishmael by Hagar, and Isaac by Sarah his wife. Isaac was born according to the promise of God when they were both grown old. Isaac feared the God of his father Abraham, and his father sent afar, and took a wife for him, even Rebecca out of his own family in Mesopotamia, because he was unwilling he should marry among the wicked Canaanites, whom God had doomed to destruction.

Isaac had by Rebecca two sons Esau and Jacob. Esau sold his birthright for a mess of pottage when he was faint with hunting: And Jacob by his mother's contrivance obtained his father's blessing. Jacob was called Israel, because he prayed and prevailed with God for a blessing. Jacob had twelve sons, and the most famous of them in sacred history were Levi, Judah, and Joseph. The priesthood in following times was committed to Levi's family. The kingdom and government
in

in future ages were promised chiefly to Judah's family.

Joseph's brethren sold him for a slave in Egypt, where he became a ruler of the land. His brethren envied him because his father loved him, and made him a coat of many colours, and because he dreamed that they should bow down to him. By a false accusation Joseph was cast into prison, and he interpreted the dreams of some of his fellow-prisoners, and, when the interpretation proved true, then he was sent for to court to interpret the king's dream about the seven years of plenty and seven years of famine.

In the famine Joseph's brethren came to buy corn in Egypt, and bowed down to him according to his dreams; but he treated them roughly at first, as a great lord and a stranger, till their conscience smote them for their former cruelty to him: But afterwards he made himself known to them with much affection and tenderness. And he manifested his forgiveness of them, for he sent for his father, and bid his children bring all their families into Egypt, and he maintained them all during the famine. Jacob and Joseph died

Of the HOLY SCRIPTURES. 19

died in Egypt, but according to their desire their bodies were carried up and buried in the land of Canaan, in faith of the promise that their seed should possess that land.

The Israelites were afterwards made slaves in Egypt, and a new king who knew not Joseph sorely oppressed them, and endeavoured to destroy them: But God heard their cry, and delivered them by the hand of Moses and Aaron. Upon Pharaoh's refusal to let the people of Israel go, they brought ten plagues upon the king and upon all the land by the authority and power of God.

At last Pharaoh released the Israelites, and the number of them that went out of Egypt were six hundred thousand men besides children, and all went on foot. When they were in distress with the Red-Sea before them and Pharaoh's army behind them, they cried unto God; whereon Moses bid them " Stand still and see the " salvation of the Lord." Then at the command of God, Moses struck the sea with his rod, and divided the waters asunder; and the children of Israel went through upon dry land. And the Egyptians

tians following, the waters returned upon them and they were drowned.

The Israelites went wheresoever God guided them by the pillar of cloud and the pillar of fire. At every new difficulty when they wanted meat or water, or met with enemies, they fell a murmuring against God and Moses: And they wandered forty years in the wilderness for their sins, before they came to the place God promised them.

While in the wilderness about three months after their coming out of Egypt, God wrote with his own hand the ten commandments in two tables of stone, and gave them to Moses. The four first commandments contained their duty to God, and the six last their duty towards men. These ten commands are called the Moral Law, and relate to their behaviour as men: And almost every thing contained in them is taught by the light of nature, and obliges all mankind. But the great end of the Jewish Ceremonies was to be emblems or types of Christ and his gospel.

The scripture gives an account of God's bringing the Israelites into the land of Canaan, under the ministration of Joshua, their government by Judges several hundred years; and after that there is a narrative of their first four kings, namely, Saul, David, Solomon and Rehoboam. In Rehoboam's days the nation was divided into two kingdoms, which were called the kingdom of Israel and the kingdom of Judah. There are also particular records of the government of these two distinct kingdoms under a long succession of their own kings, till they were both carried into captivity by the kings of Assyria.

After this the sacred history relates the return of many of them into their own land, and the rebuilding the city of Jerusalem and the temple of God, and the settlement of the affairs of church and state by Ezra and Nehemiah, which is the end of the historical part of the Old Testament.

There is also a large and particular narrative of the lives or transactions of some extraordinary persons, several of which are much interwoven with the series of the history:

history: But there are others which seem to stand separate and distinct, such are the affairs relating to Job a rich man in the east, Jonah a prophet in Israel, and Esther the queen of Persia.

We have an account of the several prophets and messengers which were sent from God on special occasions to reveal his mind and will to men: We have the writings of sixteen prophets, that is, of four greater, and twelve lesser prophets. The four great prophets are Isaiah, Jeremiah, Ezekiel, and Daniel. The twelve lesser prophets are Hoseah, Joel, Amos, Obadiah, Jonah, Micah, Nahum, Habakkuk, Zephaniah, Haggai, Zechariah, and Malachi the last prophet: He prophesied about 429 years before the coming of Christ, who assumed our nature about 4000 years after the creation of the world. God himself and his prophets, throughout all ages, foretold his coming as some great Deliverer, as the Messiah or Anointed of God.

THE chief subjects of the history of the New Testament are our Lord Jesus Christ, the great Redeemer and glorious Saviour; John the Baptist, who was his fore-

Of the HOLY SCRIPTURES.

forerunner; and the apoſtles, who were his followers.

The great Meſſiah was born at Bethlehem of the tribe of Judah according to the predictions and propheſies of him in the Old Teſtament: John the Baptiſt was his forerunner, who preached the doctrine of repentance and forgiveneſs of ſins, and directed the people to Jeſus Chriſt the Meſſiah and Saviour, " the Lamb of God who takes away the ſin of the world."

Jeſus Chriſt, the eternal Son of God, veiled his divine Glory and became man, was born of Mary, who was a virgin, according to the prophecy of Iſaiah. Jeſus, being about thirty years of age, began his miniſtry, and appeared with the marks of a divine commiſſion, and the characters of the Meſſiah upon him. He healed the ſick, he raiſed the dead, he preached the glad tidings of forgiveneſs of ſin and ſalvation to the poor, and received ſeveral teſtimonies from heaven. After he had preached his goſpel about three years and an half, he was betrayed by Judas, and ſuffered the death on the croſs, and roſe again according to the ſcriptures.

Jeſus,

Jesus, after his resurrection, appeared to his apostles, and continued on earth about forty days, and gave farther instructions in the great things of the gospel. He appointed his disciples to meet him in Galilee; he told them that all power in heaven and in earth was given into his hands; he gave them their commission to preach the gospel to all nations, and promised his presence with them, and a power to work miracles for the vindication of their doctrine. He commanded his apostles to tarry at Jerusalem till the promised Spirit should fall upon them. And on the day of Pentecost, which was ten days after the ascension of Christ, the Spirit of God was sent down upon them, and, upon their preaching of the resurrection and exaltation of Christ, three thousand souls believed, and were added to the disciples of Christ, and baptised on that day.

This was the proper beginning of the Christian or Gospel dispensation, the kingdom of Christ being set up in the world in its glory at the pouring down of the Spirit after his resurrection, and his exaltation to the government of the world and the church. The dispensation during the

Of the HOLY SCRIPTURES. 25

the life of Chrift, was a Medium between the Jewifh and Chriftian Difpenfations.

The apoftles, after Chrift's afcenfion, publifhed the gofpel he had preached, namely, pardon of fin and everlafting life to thofe that repent and believe in him, whether Jews or Gentiles, and pronounced the punifhments of hell upon the impenitent and unbelieving. The apoftles in their epiftles to the Chriftian Churches often mention the great article of the gofpel, the redemption by Chrift's death, and the atonement made for fin by his fufferings, and it fhines every where through the epiftles of St. Paul.

In the gofpels as well as epiftles faith or believing in Jefus Chrift is required as the way and method of being a partaker of the bleffings of falvation, for without faith there is no falvation according to the gofpel. This Faith unites the foul to Chrift, and makes the believer a member of Chrift's myftical body: Faith is wrought in the foul by the Spirit of God, who convinces him of the evil and danger of fin which makes him obnoxious to the law of God; and feeing no other way of help, he applies to Chrift to be his prophet, prieft,

B and

and king, and receives him as proposed in the gospel, trusts and relies upon him and his righteousness for pardon and salvation: And where this Faith is, it is attended with Repentance and Holiness, which give a meetness for heaven; and a true Faith in Jesus Christ and his righteousness may be said to entitle the believer to the heavenly kingdom. "If any man "be in Christ, he is a New Creature." Justification and sanctification are blessings connected together and graciously bestowed upon one and the same person.

The New Testament is the last dispensation of the Covenant of Grace, and it may be called New, because it is never to wax old or be abolished; and this is evident, because it concludes with a promise of Christ's second coming at the end of the world. Rev. xxii. 20. "Surely I "come quickly. Amen. Even so, come "Lord Jesus. The grace of our Lord "Jesus Christ be with us all." Amen.

London December 18, 1749.

A. C.

DIRECTIONS
FOR THE
Profitable Reading
OF THE
HOLY SCRIPTURES, &c.

The INTRODUCTION.

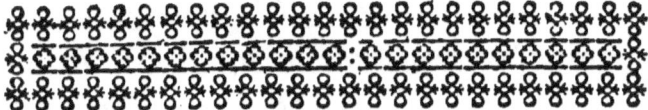UR Divines have taken a great deal of pains, both by preaching and writing, to convince men of the obligations lying upon them to read and study the Holy Scriptures; and are as induſtrious to lay before their people the great advantages they would re-

receive by reading and meditating upon God's word, as the *Romanists* have been solicitous to deter their Disciples from this employment, by representing to them the dangers they are likely to incur thereby. A great presumption, that the former are well assured that their doctrines will bear the test of the Scriptures; and the latter are conscious to themselves, that their tenets will not abide so severe a trial.

Thus far the argument in general has been sufficiently handled; but there is another particular relating to this subject, that seems not to have been much considered, and that is, *The giving rules for the more profitable reading of the Scriptures, and instructing persons, of ordinary understandings, what parts of Scripture are fittest for them to read, and best suited to their capacities.* This I take to be a consideration of great use and importance; the handling of which distinctly, would of itself contain a full answer to all those popular objections which the

the *Popish* writers have made against the promiscuous reading of the *Bible*: As if we gave authority thereby to the meanest and most ignorant people, to judge of the sense of the abstrusest and most difficult parts of God's word; and that this private interpretation of Scripture was the last resort in all disputes, from which there lay no appeal either to the ancient fathers and councils, or to the authority of the present guides and governors of the Church. From whence they infer, that whatever Heresies or Schisms arise among us, from mens rash and unwarrantable interpretations of Scripture, we ought to bear all the blame, and may thank ourselves if weak or ill-designing men turn those weapons against us, which we at first put into their hands.

But there would be no ground for these clamours, if the people were made sensible, that all parts of Scripture are not equally fitted for the capacities of all men; that as some contain *milk for babes in Christ,* so others afford *strong meat, which is proper only for those of a full* and mature *age;* that is, such as are arrived at a competent degree of knowledge in the mysteries of the Gospel; and that to understand the Scriptures throughly, so as to be able by *sound doctrine* to establish the truth, and to *convince gainsayers*, is a work that requires as good parts, and as great industry, as any study whatsoever. And therefore as the Clergy ought particularly to dedicate themselves to this employment, and bend all their studies chiefly this way, that *their lips may preserve the knowledge* of those sacred oracles; so it is the duty of the people *to seek the law at their mouths:* Not indeed to have such an implicit faith in what they say, that if they call evil good, and good evil, they should be bound to believe them; but that persons of ordinary capacities, and such have not made the study of the Scriptures their Business, should have the same deference for the judgment of their teachers in difficulties

rela-

the HOLY SCRIPTURES. 31

relating to points of religion, as thofe that never ftudied Law or Phyfic, have for the Judgment of Lawyers or Phyficians in matters relating to their feveral profeffions. ' Our Church is very
' unjuftly reproached by the Papifts,
' *to ufe the words of a learned writer* [a],
' as if it left every one at liberty to in-
' terpret Scripture as they pleafed;
' for we embrace the *ancient Creeds* as
' the fummary comprehenfion of the
' articles of our faith; and we think
' no man ought to follow his fancy,
' in rejecting any doctrines which
' have been univerfally received in the
' Chriftian Church from the times of
' the Apoftles: And in difficult cafes
' we require all men to call in the
' affiftance of their fpiritual guides
' and governors, whom God has ap-
' pointed for the better inftructing
' and governing private perfons.'

This I take to be the true ftate of the cafe, concerning the *peoples right to read and expound the Scriptures*:

[a] *Anfwer to the royal papers.*

B 4. And

And it has this fair presumption on its side, that it is equally placed between two extremes, namely, that of locking up the Scriptures, and taking the *key of knowledge* out of the peoples hands; and the other of making every ignorant mechanic a judge of the sense and meaning of the most abstruse parts of God's word. Both which opinions seem to render the pastoral office useless and insignificant: For there is no use of teachers where no body is obliged to learn (and there is little encouragement for knowledge in that church, which makes an implicit faith in her belief sufficient to salvation): And where every body sets up for that employment, what need is there of a particular order of men set apart for that purpose?

But lest any of the learned Laity should suspect that I intend to confine the knowledge of the Scriptures to the Clergy, I shall not scruple to declare, that I heartily join in that generous wish of *Moses*[a], *would God that all the Lord's people were Prophets:* And where

[a] Numb. xi. 29.

the HOLY SCRIPTURES. 33

where any of them by the advantage of a learned education, and proportionable induſtry, hath arrived to a good degree of critical ſkill in the Scriptures, I ſhall have as great regard to his judgment in thoſe matters, as to any church-man's whatſoever, neither of them being to be relied upon any further than they can ſhew that they have reaſon, the analogy of faith, and the phraſeology of Scripture on their ſide.

CHAP. I.

That the ſeveral parts of Scripture were accommodated to mens uſe, with a regard to their ſeveral capacities; which appears by the different ſubjects therein treated of, and the different ſtiles wherein the ſeveral parts of Scripture were written.

THOSE that pleaſe themſelves in raiſing cavils againſt the Holy Scriptures, do it chiefly upon this
B 5 ground;

ground; That every one would have them writ just in that stile and method, which is most suitable to his own genius. Men that are used to range their thoughts in exact method and order, expect the *Bible* should be writ like a regular system of philosophy, and are offended with the sundry repetitions they meet with there, and the want of exact order and coherence. They that do not care to be at any pains or trouble in searching the Scriptures, would have all divine truths laid down there in such plain terms, that he *that runs may read them.* The men of politeness and elegancy decry the holy books for want of a fine thread of subtle reasoning, recommended with the ornaments of wit and eloquence: So the *Greeks* sought after *wisdom* in the preaching and writings of the Apostles.

Thus every sceptic expects that Gods Spirit should comply with his fancy and humour: But the divine wisdom, instead of gratifying each particular person in his unreasonable de-

demands, has rather confulted the general profit and advantage of all together, and in the feveral parts of holy Writ *has become all things to all men*. The holy Spirit has condefcended to the weaker and more ignorant part of mankind, in that plain and unaffected ftile wherewith all neceffary truths are delivered, and often inculcated in feveral parts of Scripture, particularly in the *Gofpels*, the greateft part of the *Epiftles*, and the *practical* books of the *old Teftament*. The *parables* of our Saviour, the *typical* reprefentations of the *Jewifh œconomy*, and the *myftical* fenfe of the *prophetical* writings, will find employment fufficient, both to humble the thoughts and exercife the talents of the moft fubtle and inquifitive men. *Laftly*, That lofty and majeftic eloquence, which is fo confpicuous in feveral parts of holy Writ, particularly in the writings of the Prophets, is able to recommend itfelf to the greateft mafters of eloquence, and withal very proper to infpire the minds of attentive readers with noble ideas of the divine wisdom and providence, suitable to the greatness of those sublime truths which are there discovered to us.

If the whole body of the Scriptures had been written with that accuracy of phrase and method, which chiefly recommends human writings to the perusal of the curious, it would not have answered one great intent and design of it, which was to *give wisdom to the simple and* unlearned. If there had been nothing of abstruseness in the things there treated of, or in the manner of expressing them, it would hardly have detained the thoughts of the curious, or rewarded the industry of the diligent. But God has so wisely tempered those different qualities together, that he who has much understanding will find employment for his best thoughts in searching out the *deep things of God's word*; and he that has but little, may learn enough from thence to make him wise unto salvation.

The

The several parts of Scripture being thus adapted to mens several capacities, it plainly follows from hence, that he who would read the Scriptures with profit, must begin with the plainest books first, and make them the chief subject of his reading and meditation, and not meddle with the obscure and difficult parts of holy Writ, 'till he is very well vers'd in the former. This is the natural method and order to be used in all sorts of learning, to begin with the plainest things first; and therefore they that are *unskilful in the word of righteousness, and have need of milk, and not of strong meat,* should not be too forward to busy their heads with the more abstruse parts of God's word, but should content themselves with studying the plainest books first, 'till they become perfect masters of those writings, which as they are easiest to be understood, so they afford the greatest matter of edification to all attentive readers. Such are, as I observed before, the greatest part of the *new Testament*, and *Psalms*, and practical books

books of the *old*. And yet we find it a common fault, and that which the weakest and most injudicious people are usually most guilty of, *namely*, that they neglect the reading those books of Holy Scripture which deliver, with great plainness and perspicuity, all things necessary for a Christian to know and practise, and perplex themselves with the more abstruse parts of the *Bible*, of such as are the prophecies of *Daniel*, *Ezekiel*, and the *Revelation*, which can afford but small edification to unlearned and ignorant readers, but by being misunderstood, or misapplied, may lead them into great and dangerous mistakes. Accordingly experience has given us many examples of unlearned and unsettled heads, who by this means have lost not only the true sense of religion, but even their common sense and judgment as to other matters, have fancied themselves designed by God to be his instruments in fulfilling of prophecies, and thought themselves dispensed with from observing

the HOLY SCRIPTURES. 39

serving the ordinary duties of fearing God and keeping his commandments, because they were made choice of to serve him in the extraordinary way of overturning kingdoms and unsettling governments.

I doubt not but wise and sober men may make a very good use of the more abstruse parts of God's word, as I shall farther shew in the sequel of this discourse. God gives some men a peculiar insight into deep and mysterious truths, and furnishes them with particular talents for that purpose: *He opens the eyes* of their understanding, that *they may see the wondrous things of his word,* as a reward of their laborious search and pious thirst after divine knowledge: As he did not think fit to [a] *hide from Abraham the thing he was about to do.* So that to say, as some have done, that the *reading of the Revelation either finds men mad, or makes them so,* is, in the first place, a very rash and bold censure of a book, which

[a] Gen. xviii. 17.

which all Christians acknowledge to have been writ by divine inspiration; and then a very odd comment upon the very frontispiece and introduction to it, which says, [b] *Blessed is he that readeth, and they that hear the words of this Prophecy.* But what I insist upon at present, is this, that when persons of weak and unsettled minds pass over the plain books of Scripture, and will be too prying into the obscure parts of it, it looks like the presumption of *Uzzah*, and the men of *Bethshemesh*, [c] who approached the ark with too much curiosity; and it is commonly attended with as bad a consequence; it makes a *breach* both into their understandings and their morals. St. *Paul* indeed says, [d] that *all Scripture is profitable*; but he does not say it is so to all men, but particularly to *the man of God*, to the teachers of the Church, as the context plainly restrains the words. The primitive Church cannot be accused

[b] Rev. 1. 3.   [c] 1 Sam. vi. 19. 2 Sam. vi. 7.
[d] 2 Tim. iii. 16, 17.

the HOLY SCRIPTURES. 41

cufed of encouraging ignorance in the people, and yet *Origen* [e] informs us, that there was a diftinction made then between thofe books of Scripture which lay open to every body's ufe, and fuch as were read only by perfons of better underftandings: A diftinction, which if it had been obferved in thefe latter ages, would have not a little contributed to the peace of the Church.

I am fenfible fome may think it too rigorous an injunction, abfolutely to forbid ordinary perfons the reading the more abftrufe parts of the *Bible*; and it is likely that feveral will not ftick to call it a *Popifh* doctrine, and defigned for the introducing implicit faith, and blind obedience. Therefore to prevent fuch a mifconftruction, I fhall, in the purfuit of this argument, not only give directions for the profitable reading of the

---

[e] L. 7. c. Celf. p. 356. Οὐκ ἐν ἀνακεχωρηκόσι τὰ ἀναγινωσκομένοις ὑπὸ ὀλίγων μόνον καὶ φιλομαθῶν, ἀλλ' ἐν τοῖς δημωδεστέροις γέγραπται, ὅτι τὰ ἀόρατα τοῦ Θεοῦ, &c. Rom. i. 20.

plainer

plainer parts of the Holy Scriptures, but likewise consider what use persons of common capacities may, and ought to make of the obscurer books of the *Bible*. The handling which subject will have this benefit in it, that it may prevent mens making an ill use of those sacred writings, and thereby raising an evil report against them.

CHAP. II.

Two prejudices which hinder many from the careful reading and study of the Scriptures. The first of them, relating to the stile and method of those holy writings, considered.

NOT only the enemies of our holy religion have raised several objections against the stile of the Scriptures, but some well-disposed persons have neglected to read them, because they thought they could be better edified and instructed by the prac-

the HOLY SCRIPTURES. 43

practical writings of private divines, where they find their duty laid down in an easier method, and with greater plainness and perspicuity of expression.

Before I give a particular answer to this difficulty, I shall premise in general, that supposing the utmost of this objection were true, yet we ought to come to God with the same simplicity of mind and resignation of judgment, that every learner brings with him, when he comes to his master; and it is fit we should pay that deference to his wisdom, as intirely to submit to what method of instruction he thinks most proper for us. And we may reasonably believe, that God will particularly bless the endeavours of those that thus come to him in his own way, and acquiesce in those means of instruction which he himself has ordained: Besides, there is a majesty and authority in the word of God, which is not to be found in human writings; and when we hear God speak unto us, sometimes by his Prophets, sometimes by his Apostles,

some-

sometimes by his Son, and sometimes by himself, this must needs affect us with extraordinary reverence; and we cannot chuse but give the same earnest heed to the things thus spoken to us, as we would to a voice that came from heaven.

Having premised thus much in general, I proceed to give a more particular answer to the objection, and shall endeavour to vindicate the stile and method of writing used by the sacred penmen, by shewing, that it affords several arguments to prove the truth and certainty of the things contained in the Scriptures; as will appear from these four considerations.

1. *As to the historical books of Scripture, the principal matters are there recorded with such circumstances, that they mutually confirm and support each other.*

2. *If we take a general view of the whole body of Scripture, we find one and the same design carried on by several writers, who could not be supposed to combine*

bine together, since the greatest part of them lived at a considerable distance of time from each other.

3. We find the mystery of our redemption, the principal subject of the Holy Scriptures, opened there by degrees, according to the capacities and exigences of several ages.

4. That plain and inartificial manner of writing which the holy penmen use, affords weighty arguments to prove their truth and sincerity.

1. As to the historical books of Scripture, the principal matters are there recorded with such circumstances, that they do mutually confirm and support each other. To make this out by instancing in a few particulars. The history of *Abraham* and his posterity, the preferring *Isaac* before *Ishmael*, and *Jacob* before *Esau*, their sojourning in *Egypt*, and deliverance from thence, their settling in the land of *Canaan*, and the account which we have of their several idolatries

tries and captivities afterwards. These passages of the sacred story contain in them a signal accomplishment of the promises made to *Abraham*, of the prophecies uttered by *Jacob* upon his death-bed, and the predictions of *Moses* before he left the world. We are further to consider, that these historical accounts are mixt and interwoven with several particulars relating to the affairs of the neighbouring nations, *namely*, the *Ishmaelites, Egyptians, Edomites*, &c. which we cannot suspect that the sacred writers would forge; for that would have been to expose themselves to the scorn and reproach of their professed enemies.

The same writings do likewise inform us, that the settlement of the *Jews* in the land of *Canaan*, their form of government, their customs and manner of life, were nothing else but the putting the laws of *Moses* in execution; many of which being burdensome and chargeable, we cannot suppose a whole nation would have voluntarily submitted to them,

them, without pregnant proofs of their divine authority.

In like manner, if we view the history of the Gospels, we may observe that it contains several predictions, concerning the destruction of *Jerusalem*, the rejecting of the *Jews*, the calling of the *Gentiles*, the speedy propagation of the christian religion; all which, and several other prophecies there recorded, are interwoven with the thread of the Gospel history, and delivered with such circumstances as plainly shew those histories to be writ several years before the events so foretold did come to pass.

These considerations afford a full answer to those that find fault with the Scripture as confused and immethodical: To whom it is a sufficient reply to say, that the historical, prophetical, and doctrinal parts of the *Bible* are so mixt and interwoven together, because they mutually add strength to each other: The histories shew the completion of the prophecies; the prophecies confirm the truth of the histories;

ries; and both of them prove the divine authority of the doctrine.

2. *The harmony and agreement between the several writers of the old and new Testament, tho' the greatest part of them lived at a considerable distance from each other, is a convincing proof of their truth and sincerity.*

Some that take upon them to prescribe to God Almighty, how he should reveal his will to the world, would have all the prophecies concerning our Saviour's birth, life, sufferings, and exaltation, comprized under one collection; and have all saving truth reduced into one system. But those correctors of the *Bible* do not consider, that by this means we should lose one very considerable argument, for the truth and divine authority of the Scriptures, which is taken from the harmony and agreement of the inspired writers, tho' they lived in distant ages, and writ upon different occasions. The writings of the *old* and
new

new Testament, like two faithful witnesses, verify and confirm each other's testimony: What the *old Testament* promises, the *new* performs: What the one foretells, the other represents the accomplishment of. Several books of the Scripture Canon were writ at a great distance of time from each other, and consequently by persons that could hold no correspondence together, some of them living near two thousand years asunder. This proves that is was impossible they could conspire to put a cheat upon the world; and from thence it follows, that the religion contained in the *old* and *new Testament*, could not be a piece of human contrivance, since the several authors of those books could never combine together in carrying on such a design.

The Apostles were so well satisfied, that what they taught was agreeable to the doctrine of the *old Testament*, that they still appeal to those writings upon all occasions; and tho' they testified nothing but *what they had seen and heard*, yet they thought it
added

added great weight to their testimony, that they [a] *said no other things than what* Moses *and the Prophets did say should come.* The miraculous gifts they were endowed with, were an undeniable proof of their divine commission: But yet St. *Peter* calls the predictions contained in the *old Testament*, [c] *A more sure word of prophecy;* as if it were in some respects a more convincing proof of the truth of Christianity, than miracles themselves. Both the miracles, and the persons who wrought them, were necessarily confined to one particular time and place; whereas the sundry prophecies concerning the *Messias* and his kingdom, which are scattered up and down throughout the *old Testament*, are the united suffrage of several ages of the world, and contain the concurring testimony of men, who could never join in carrying on one common interest or design, and agreed in nothing but in uttering those divine truths, which they all received from

[a] Acts xxvi. 22.   [c] 2 Pet. i. 19.

one

one and the same spirit. This consideration leads me to the

3. Particular, wherein the wisdom of God appears in the manner of his inditing the Holy Scriptures, namely, *In the different steps and degrees whereby the mystery of our redemption is unfolded by the sacred writers.*

This indeed is but a continuance of the former argument, and a fuller discovery of the harmony and agreement of the several writers of the *old Testament:* In that they all pursue one and the same great design, which is to foretel and describe the coming of the *Messias,* the foundation of all divine revelation, and preserve in mens minds an earnest expectation of his appearance.

And here I shall briefly consider the different steps whereby this great truth was discovered to the Patriarchs *before the law,* to *Moses* in *the ordinances*

nances of the law, and to the Prophets *afterwards*.

Immediately upon the fall of our firſt parents, God, who *in the midſt of judgment remembers mercy*, comforted them under their deſponding apprehenſions, by giving them the promiſe *of the ſeed of the woman, which ſhould break the ſerpent's head*, by whom they had been betrayed into ſin and miſery.

To *Abraham* God afterwards more fully revealed, that the *promiſed ſeed*, or *Meſſias*, ſhould ariſe out of his family, ^e *In thy ſeed ſhall all the nations of the earth be bleſſed.* To *Jacob* it was ſhewed, that he ſhould ſpring from the tribe of *Judah*, and come into the world before the *Scepter ſhould depart from* that tribe.

Under *Moſes*, the deliverance of the *Iſraelites* from the *Egyptian* bondage, and all the rites and ſacrifices ordained by his miniſtry, had a particular relation to that deliverance which

^e Gen. xxii. 18.

the *Meſſias* ſhould obtain for us from ſin and death, and were ſo many *figures of him that was to come.*

The Prophets that ſucceeded, plac'd this truth ſtill in a clearer light, by the many illuſtrious predictions which they gave concerning Chriſt's birth, family, ſufferings, reſurrection, aſcenſion, and kingdom. And by their pointing out the ſeveral circumſtances relating to the times of the *Meſſias*, and withal exhorting men not to reſt in the bare letter of the law, but to fulfil the righteouſneſs chiefly intended by it, they prepared mens minds to expect a new and better ſtate of things, a new covenant, *eſtabliſhed upon better promiſes.*

And when the Prophets had thus prepared the way for the reception of the *Meſſias*, the gift of prophecy in a great meaſure ceaſed [f], neither was there any public ſucceſſion of Prophets for the ſpace of four hundred

---

[f] *See* 1 Macc. iv. 46. ix. 27. xv. 41. Ecclus. xxxvi. 15.

years

years together, before the coming of Chrift, on purpofe to raife in mens minds a more earneft expectation of thofe happy days, wherein God had promifed to *pour out his fpirit upon all flefh*, and to afford the world greater meafures of grace and knowledge, than ever it enjoyed before.

Having thus taken a brief view of the different fteps by which God vouchfafed to make known this fundamental truth by the holy writers, we may leave it to any confidering man to determine, which of the two ways is moft ferviceable to the main end and defign of prophecy, which was to prepare the way of the *Meffias*; either for God fummarily to have fore-fhewn all the particulars relating to the times of the *Meffias* in one fingle prophecy, which is fome mens unreafonable demand, or elfe to have ufed that method he has already pitched upon, whereby the coming of Chrift is not only in exprefs words foretold by all the Prophets, but likewife myftically implied in all the

rites

the HOLY SCRIPTURES. 55

rites and ceremonies of the *Jewish* worship, and typically represented in the lives and actions of the most famous men of foregoing times. It is evident that this latter way introduces Christ into the world with a great deal more of previous solemnity, whilst it makes all the eminent men of former ages so many harbingers of his coming, and raises in mens minds a just veneration for the gospel state, as the master-piece of the divine providence, that point wherein all the lines of *God's manifold wisdom* do meet as in their center; all which is a plain demonstration, that Christ was *ordained by God before the beginning of the world*, * though in his wise disposal he did not appear until the latter ages of it.

4. *That plain and inartificial style which the holy writers make use of, affords weighty arguments to prove their truth and sincerity.*

* Tit. i. 2. 1 Pet. i. 20.

In the first place it would be absurd to expect, that part of Holy Scripture, which consists in giving laws to mankind, should be fine and persuasive: "Whereas the language "of law should be short and plain, "and full of authority, as an emi- "nent divine has observed ᶠ: Thus "we find it is among men, and "surely it is much fitter for God to "speak thus to men, than for men "to one another." ᵍ

Likewise in histories and narratives, the plainness and simplicity of the style is a great proof of the truth and sincerity of the writer. Now the plainness of the Scripture history is truly admirable; for it is joined with such a native grandeur and authority as commands an assent, and works more powerfully upon the minds of men, than all the art in the world. Without question *Moses* was able to

---

ᶠ *Arch-Bp.* Tillotf. 2*d Serm. on* Mat. xi. 2.

ᵍ *Sunt certa Legum verba, & quo plus authoritatis habeant, paulo antiquiora.* Cic. l. 2. de Legibus.

describe

describe the passions to the life, and understood the beauties of history, as well as the politest writers among the *Greeks* or *Romans*. To be convinced of this, we need only read his description of *Abraham*'s going to sacrifice his son; and the several passions *Joseph* and his brethren were affected with, at their interview in *Egypt*. Yet we may observe, that that part of his history, which himself was an eye-witness of, is written after the plainest and most inartificial manner that can be imagined, in the nature of a journal, as if he had only set down an account of every day's transactions just after they happened. Some perhaps may censure this as a careless and immethodical way of writing; but it has this great advantage in it, that the very form and style of the work shews that it has been transmitted down to us just as *Moses* wrote it.

To give his readers an undeniable proof of his impartiality, this holy writer neither conceals his own infirmities,

mities, nor any of those particulars which might reflect upon the honour of his nation, tribe, or family. He records the curse which *Jacob* pronounced at his death upon his own tribe of *Levi:* He vilifies his own birth, by acquainting us that he was born of such a marriage as his own law condemns for incestuous: He represents his nation as a stubborn, untractable people, neither to be wrought upon by God's mercies, nor his judgments.

The like air of sincerity runs thro' the whole gospel history, where the Evangelists publish, without any reserve, their own and their brethrens infirmities, their slowness of understanding, their incredulity, their little contentions among themselves; they conceal not that one of Christ's desciples betrayed his master, another denied him, and all fled from him.

If there be any such thing as *internal marks* of the truth of any history, or such arguments as are taken from the very texture and composure of the

the HOLY SCRIPTURES. 59

the work itself, as all critics acknowledge that there are, we must confess that the Scripture history has more of self-evident truth, than any history in the world.

We may further take notice upon this head, that the practical books of Scripture are written in a plain and simple style, yet without being flat and insipid: They deliver the weightiest truths in a grave and serious manner, without an affected fineness, or studied periods: They convey into our minds worthy ideas of God, and just notions of our duty, without descending to useless subtilties, or soaring too much above the apprehensions of the vulgar, which made the writings of the Philosophers of no use to far the greater part of mankind. *The words of the Lord are pure words*, as the *Psalmist* speaks, that is, they have none of that dross or alloy of error or passion, which insensibly slides into all human composures: They deliver divine truths pure and unmixt, though in a popular and inartificial manner of expreſſion, and in ſuch a way as is worthy of the majeſty of God, and yet condeſcends to the weakneſs of the generality of men.

Some indeed have objected againſt this plainneſs of the ſacred writers, as if it had betrayed them into an unbecoming extreme, and made them ſet down ſuch particulars as were not worthy to be taken notice of by a grave and wiſe hiſtorian. But ſuch perſons would do well to conſider, that when they paſs this cenſure upon particular paſſages in holy Writ, they do it by a very imperfect light: for they are not acquainted with all the circumſtances and conſequences of thoſe particulars, which are but ſlightly mentioned in Scripture: And they likewiſe judge of the ſmall importance of theſe matters by ſuch notions and opinions as prevail in their own times, without comparing them with the ſentiments of the age wherein thoſe things were tranſacted,

the HOLY SCRIPTURES. 61

acted, or inquiring whether the sacred writers might not have some further prospect in recording such matters, than they are aware of. And this, learned men have made out, as to several passages which seem light and inconsiderable, and have fully vindicated the credit and authority of the sacred writers against the cavils of this objection [a]. It was likewise an opinion received among the ancient writers, (See *Justin Martyr, Dial. c. Tryph.* p. 364, 371.) that many of the actions of the patriarchs were *typical*, or representations of the future state of the Church; which notion is very much confirmed by that passage in St. *Paul, Gal.* iv. 30. where he supposes *Abraham's casting out the bond-woman and her Son* out of his house, to presignify the ejecting of the *Jews* out of the Church of Christ.

---

[a] *See particularly Dr.* Allix's *Reflexions,* Vol. I. Part. I. Chap. 13, 15, 16. *And* Part II. Chap. 20.

These objectors would shew much more candor and impartiality, if they would not pass so hasty a censure upon such passages of holy Writ, as seem to them liable to exception; but rather say as the Philosopher did when he gave his opinion concerning the writings of *Heraclitus, What I understand is excellent; and, I presume, what I understand not, to be so too.*

CHAP. III.

An answer to another popular objection against the reading of the Scriptures, taken from their obscurity; and some rules laid down to remedy this difficulty.

ANOTHER difficulty which discourages many from reading the Scriptures, is the obscurity of several phrases and passages therein contained, which hinders them from being so instructive as books originally written in the vulgar language are; and likewise makes them liable
to

the HOLY SCRIPTURES. 63

to be perverted and misunderstood; the consequences of which are so dangerous, that some think this alone a sufficient reason why persons of ordinary capacities should not be too curious in searching the Scriptures.

In answer to this objection, I shall consider, in the first place, how far it may be charged upon the Scripture; or, in what sense the Scriptures may be esteemed obscure.

2. I shall assign the immediate causes of that obscurity.

3. I shall offer some rules, which may help to clear up the difficulties we meet with in the holy writings.

First, I shall consider, how far this objection may be charged upon the Scriptures.

Although we acknowledge there are *some things* in Scripture *hard to be understood*, yet still we affirm, that all things necessary for us to believe and practise, in order to our salvation, are

are delivered there with the greatest clearness and perspicuity. Some of the prophets indeed describe their writings as a book *sealed up,* ᵐ and not to be opened or understood by every body. But the generality of the holy writers affect great plainness of expression, and make use of a popular style, on purpose to condescend to vulgar capacities. St. *Paul* tells the *Corinthians* ⁿ, That he *used great plainness of speech, that they might all with open face,* without any veil or covering, *behold, as in a glass, the glories of the Lord.* The design of all writing is to convey our thoughts intelligibly to others; and it would be a great reflexion upon God's wisdom, if a book written by his direction, and for the instruction of mankind, should fall short of that end which human composures do generally attain to. The disputes that have risen concerning the sense of Scripture, is not always owing to

---

ᵐ Isai. xxix. 12. Dan. viii. 26. xii. 4. Rev. x. 4.
ⁿ 2 Cor. iii. 12, 18.

the

the HOLY SCRIPTURES. 65

the obfcurity of the Scripture expref-, fions; as may appear in feveral inftances: That the *death of Chrift is a propitiatory facrifice for our fins*, is as fully afferted as words can do it: In like manner, there are no plainer texts in the *Bible* than thofe that forbid the *worſhip of images*, or the *performing the public fervice in an unknown language:* The fame may be affirmed of the command of *receiving the cup in the Lord's fupper:* And yet we fee the contrary opinions and practices are maintained with as much ftiffneſs and obftinacy, as if the authority of the Scriptures were clear on the other fide. But then it is to be confeffed, that there are feveral doubts relating to particular texts, which arife either from the darkneſs and ambiguity of the phrafes and expreffions therein made ufe of, or from the obfcurity of the matters which are there handled. Thefe two are the immediate caufes of the obfcurity we meet with in the holy
Scrip-

Scripture, which I propofed to confider in the fecond place.

As to the former of thefe, namely, the obfcurity of Scripture phrafes, we are to confider that we have but a very imperfect knowledge of the language in which the *Old Teftament* was written ; and it cannot be expected but that in a book writ fo many years ago, there muft be allufions to cuftoms and tranfactions, the memory of which is worn out by length of time; and feveral expreffious made ufe of which are different from the genius and modes of fpeaking ufed in modern languages. For example, we have but few remains of antiquity to inform us what were the idolatrous cuftoms of thofe early ages, and yet it is very probable that they gave occafion to fome precepts of the ceremonial law, one great defign of which was to preferve the *Jews* from falling into the idolatries of their neighbouring nations. In like manner, if we were exactly acquainted with the method which the ancient

ent *Jews* ufed in computing their time, and the manner of their intercalations, it would, no doubt, very much contribute to clear feveral difficulties in Scripture chronology.

In the next place, the obfcurity which we find in Scripture, arifes from the things themfelves therein treated of, feveral of which are too much above our narrow capacities fully to comprehend and explain: Such as are, the nature and attributes of God, his counfels and providence, the nature of our own fouls, and the methods God hath made ufe of to recover them out of mifery. It is, I think, acknowledged on all fides, that our capacities are but finite, which very term implies that our underftanding has bounds fet to it which it cannot pafs: And fince it is thus limited, if any thing be above its reach, certainly the infinite perfections of almighty God, his ways and judgments, have the greateft reafon to be efteemed fo. Notwithftanding this, we are to take notice, that

that there may be, and certainly are, several plain propositions laid down in Scripture concerning these matters, tho' the things themselves, in their utmost extent, are above our understanding: For instance, these propositions, *God is a Spirit,* or *is eternal,* are very plain and intelligible propositions, though we cannot precisely define what a *Spirit* is, nor have any adequate notion of *Eternity.* In like manner, the Scripture does plainly affirm, that the divine nature is communicated from the *Father,* to the *Son* and *Holy Ghost,* although the manner of this communication be above our comprehension.

The obscurity, which is generally spread over the writings of the prophets, is partly owing to the forementioned causes, but is chiefly to be ascribed to providential reasons. If men could see clearly to the end of prophecies, and the manner how they were to be accomplished, they could not be brought to pass in a way either suitable to the holiness of God,

God, or to the free-will of men, who are the great inftruments of providence. The meafures whereby God governs the world, make it requifite that men fhould not be able to fathom his counfels, or know what work he has in hand: And it is abfolutely neceffary, that the methods of providence fhould be fecret and concealed from us, to make them righteous and holy in themfelves. So that what St. *Paul* fpeaks to the *Jews*, concerning the accomplifhment of thofe prophecies, which relate to the fufferings of the Meffias, may be fitly applied to the fulfilling of prophecies in general [a], *becaufe they knew him not, nor yet the voices of the prophets, they have fulfilled them in condemning him.* But having elfewhere [b] difcourfed at large concerning the providential reafons of the obfcurity of the prophetical writings, I fhall not hear repeat what has been there fpoken upon this head, and

[a] Acts xiii. 27.
[b] *Anfw. to Five Letters*, Ch. 4.

fhall

shall only add, that several reasons may be assigned, why God should suffer some things in other parts of the holy Scriptures to be obscure. We are apt to despise what is plain and easy; upon which account, as the obscurity of some passages in Scripture is very proper to humble us before God, and teach us to adore those depths of the divine wisdom, which are contained in his word; so it is a means to excite our industry in searching out divine truth, and make us receive it with joy, when we have discovered it [d]. Our value for Scripture knowledge is increased by the labour we took in finding it out; and our pains are abundantly recompensed in the satisfaction which devout souls feel in the discoveries which God makes to them of himself. *They rejoice in Spirit*, as our Saviour did upon the like occasion [e], and heartily *thank* their

[d] *Sunt in scripturis S. profunda mysteria, quæ ad hoc absconduntur ne vilescant, ad hoc quæruntur, ut exerceant.* August.
[e] Luke x. 21.

hea-

the HOLY SCRIPTURES. 71
heavenly *Father for revealing that truth which he hides from the worldly-wife, to babes in Chrift,* to thofe that hunger and thirft after righteoufnefs, and efteem the knowledge and love of God to be the chiefeft part of human felicity.

I proceed, in the third place, to offer fome general rules or directions, for clearing up the difficulties we meet with in Scriptures, and enabling us to read them with profit.

And in the firft place I premife that it is abfolutely neceffary, that perfons of ordinary education and capacities fhould depend upon the judgment of thofe teachers and inftructors which God has placed over them, for the fenfe of difficult places of Scripture.

I readily acknowledge that there are fome things fo plainly delivered in Scripture, that no authority in the world can oblige men to doubt of their fenfe and meaning : Such is the fenfe of the fecond commandment, in direct terms forbidding the *worſhip of*
ima-

images; and the command of our Saviour's exprefsly requiring all his difciples to partake of the *cup in the Lord's fupper*. In thefe and fuch like cafes, a perfon of common fenfe may fafely keep clofe to the letter of the Scripture, though it be in oppofition to the greateft confent of human authority. But what I here lay down, I would have underftood with relation to a great many other controverfies of religion, where perfons of mean capacities are not able to judge of the force of a good argument, much lefs of the iffue of a long difpute. And in thefe cafes, I affirm their beft fecurity is to rely upon the judgment of thofe teachers, whom providence and their fuperiors have placed over them.

I fhall not fcruple to affirm, that there never was a greater piece of enthufiafm broached than this, that men may be fufficiently qualified for expofitors of Scripture, without the help of ftudy or human learning. It is granted, that the Scriptures are plain in neceffary things; but no book can

can be so plain, but that it is requisite for the perfect understanding of it, that men should be acquainted with the idioms and proprieties of the original language, and the customs and notions which were generally received at the time when it was writ.

This is a difficulty common to Scripture, with all other books of antiquity: And they that in either case cannot inform themselves in these matters, which require some skill in ancient learning, must rely upon the judgment of those who have made those studies their business and profession. The meanest artificer thinks his trade and mystery not to be learned without serving an apprenticeship; and yet many of those very persons fancy the profession of Divinity requires neither parts nor industry. This is a piece of presumption as old as the times of St. *Jerom*ⁿ, (though very

---

ⁿ *Sola scripturarum ars est, quam sibi omnes passim vendicant —— Hanc garrula anus, hanc delirus senex, hanc sophista verbosus, hanc universi præsumunt.*

much increased by the licentiousness of latter times) who complains, "That the sense of the Scriptures was the only piece of knowledge, which every one thought himself a competent judge of, without pains or study, without the help of a guide or instructor." St. *Peter* tells us, [*] that *unlearned and unstable men did wrest the Scriptures* in his time, without any regard to the authority of the Apostles themselves, who were infallible interpreters of the holy oracles: But he adds, that *it was their own destruction*, and that justly; for since God has appointed pastors in his Church to be guides to the people, if they, through pride or obstinacy, will despise instruction, it is their own fault *if they fall into the ditch.*

And this, by the way, may convince men of ordinary capacities, that it is much safer for them to err

---

lacerant, docent antequam discant. Hieron. Epist. ad Paulin. init. Tom. 3.

[*] 2 Pet. iii. 16.

with the established Church, than to err by being of a party against it: So that the scruples of our separatists are still on the *wrong side*, as a great man [e], who was far from being their enemy, hath justly stated their case, all of them against government and obedience, none of them in favour of two things so necessary to the preservation of all society. When men err with their governors, they have this favourable plea on their side, that they were led into error by those whom God had placed over them: But when men forsake the truth and the Church together, both these faults will be laid to their charge; First, leaving the truth, and embracing error; and then causelessly breaking the peace of the Church. It were well, if this matter were seriously considered by many now-a-days, who are apt to think their souls are then in the safest condition, when they are at the

---

[e] *Archbishop* Tillotson's *Sermon upon* Acts xxiv. 16. p. 384. *Edit. Fol.*

greatest distance from the established Church.

Having premised this necessary caution concerning the submission and deference due to the judgment of our spiritual guides in expounding Scripture; I proceed to lay down more particular rules and directions for the right understanding and interpretation of it.

The first rule I shall offer is this, *That we would begin with reading the plainest books first.* This advice I have recommended already [f], and shall only add, to what has been said there upon this head, that I take the *Gospels* to be one of the most proper books for any person to begin with, that designs to make a good progress in Scripture knowledge. For these are plain and easy, and generally intelligible to the meanest capacity, and yet must needs afford extraordinary edification to those that will give attendance to the reading of them. For here we have him speak unto us, who came down

[f] Chap. i.

from

from heaven on purpose that he might instruct us, and teach us the way of God more perfectly: We have him speak unto us, *who spake as never man did.* And because example is of greater force than bare precept, we have his doctrine set forth to the life, in his most glorious example, and holy conversation.

Next to the Gospels, I would recommend the reading of the book of *Psalms,* as being the great treasure of spiritual devotion, and very proper to raise in our souls devout affections of faith and hope toward God, of love and thankfulness to him, of reverence to his name and word, and submission to his will and providence.

I shall conclude this particular with the excellent directions St. *Jerom* gives to *Læta,* in his epistle to her concerning the education of her daughter, where speaking of this subject, he advises her *first to teach her* daughter the Psalms, *and let her,* saith he, *be entertained with these holy songs: Then let her be instructed in the common*

duties

78 DIRECTIONS *for reading*
duties of life by the Proverbs *of* Solomon. *Let her learn from* Eccléſiaſtes, *to deſpiſe worldly things; tranſcribe from* Job *the practice of patience and virtue: Let her paſs then to the* Goſpels, *and never let them be out of her hands; and then imbibe with all the faculties of her mind the* Acts *and* Epiſtles. *When ſhe has enriched the ſtore-houſe of her breaſt with thoſe treaſures, let her learn the books of* Moſes, Joſhua, *and* Judges, *the books of* Kings *and* Chronicles, *the volumes of* Ezra *and* Eſther; *and laſtly the* Canticles.

2. The ſecond rule I would offer to this purpoſe, is, *To have a regard to the analogy of faith, in the reading and interpreting the Scriptures.*

This is the Apoſtle's rule, *Rom.* xii. 6. *If any man propheſy* (which word often ſignifies explaining and interpreting Scripture in the writings of the *new Teſtament*) *let him propheſy according to the analogy or proportion of faith.*
This

the HOLY SCRIPTURES. 79

This rule equally holds with refpect to thofe that inftruct, as well as thofe that learn. It implies having always a regard to the fundamental principles both of faith and practice, and never interpreting any particular text of Scripture in fuch a fenfe as to make it contradict any of thofe fundamental points of doctrine or good manners, which we find often repeated in the Holy Scriptures, and every where the greateft ftrefs laid upon them.

To this purpofe St. *John* ᵍ lays down this rule for *trying the fpirits,* that is, thofe doctrines which were taught by men pretending to the fpirit : *Every fpirit that confeffeth not that Jefus Chrift is come in the flefh, is not of God.* This was a fundamental principle of Chriftianity, by which other doctrines were to be tried. St. *Paul* lays down a rule to the fame purpofe,ʰ *If any man teach otherwife, and confent not to wholfome words, and to the doctrine which is according to godlinefs,* that is, if any man teach fuch doctrines as

ᵍ 1 John iv. 1, 2.   ʰ 1 Tim. vi. 3.

D 4   con-

contradict the main design of Christianity, which was to promote true holiness, they are not to be hearkened to, nor is the sense which they give of any particular text of Scripture to be received; because it contradicts the chief design of Religion in general and of Christianity in particular, which plainly tells us, That *Christ came into the world to destroy the works of the devil* [d], *and gave himself for us that he might redeem us from all antiquity, and purify unto himself a peculiar people, zealous of good works* [e].

For instance, if any one interpret those texts of Scripture which maintain our *justification by faith only*, or our *salvation by free grace*, to such a sense as excludes the necessity of *good works*, such an interpretation is to be rejected, because it contradicts the main design of Christianity, which was to *make us holy as God is holy* [f], and *cleanse us from all filthiness both of flesh and spi-*

[d] 1 John iii. 8. [e] Tit. ii. 14. [f] 1 Pet. i. 15.

rit [g].

rit [g]. This doctrine is so often and plainly insisted upon by the holy writers, that the number and evidence of Scripture authority, as to this point, ought in all reason to over-balance [h] any argument drawn from a few obscure passages, that may seem at first sight to look another way. For this rule ought inviolably to be observed in judging of the sense of Scripture, *never to interpret an obscure text in such a sense, as to make it contradict a plain one* [i]. For certainly we must judge of what is obscure from what is plain; not on the contrary; because the rule whereby we judge ought to be more known than the thing is upon which we are to pass our judgment. And yet this is the usual method of those who main-

[g] 2 Cor. vii. 1.
[h] *Regula omni rei semper ab initio constituta ex pluribus in pauciora præscribit.* Tertull. adverf. Praxeam. c. 20.
[i] *Inhærendum est iis quæ in scriptura sunt aperta, ut exiis revelentur obscura.* August. de Merit. Peccat. l. 3. c. 4.

tain some singular conceit or opinion: If they can find but one passage of Scripture that seems to countenance it, they presently lay hold of that, and will hardly give a fair hearing to any other texts, how plain soever, that might help to expound this single passage, and set it in it's true light.

3. The third rule I would recommend for this purpose, *To compare one place of Scripture with another.*

This rule St. *Paul* has likewise recommended to us by his own practice, [k] *We speak,* saith he, *not in the words which man's wisdom teacheth, comparing spiritual things with spiritual.* Not to exclude any other helps for understanding the holy text from their due usefulness, it is a common, and true observation, that *Scripture doth*

[k] 1 Cor. ii. 12.

best interpret itself. This we may assign, as one reason, why the *Bible* is not writ with an exact order, or the artificial method of a system of Divinity; but the same truths are often repeated and inculcated over again. This neglect of art and method may perhaps give offence to some overnice palates; but it is really of great use, especially to common readers. The very repeating of weighty truths makes a deeper impression upon ordinary understandings; what is obscurely delivered in one place, is more clearly expressed in another; and what is figuratively set forth in the *old Testament*, is more plainly laid down in the *new*. And in this case the comparing the prediction with the event, does not only add new light to the former, but moreover the holy writers thereby mutually confirm each other's testimony. The comparing one text of Scripture with another, is further useful upon several accounts.

1. This

1. This method doth acquaint us with the peculiar phrafes of Scripture, and forms of fpeech which are proper to thofe languages wherein the Scriptures were written, by which means we learn how to reconcile feveral texts that feem to contradict each other. So the doctrine of St. *Paul* and St. *James* concerning *juftification by faith*, may be eafily reconciled by obferving the different acceptations of the word *faith* in the holy writers.

2. From hence, in the next place, we learn in what fenfe we are to underftand feveral *metaphorical* expreffions which we meet with in the facred writings. For inftance; God is often defcribed there as having hands and eyes, ears, and bowels, and other parts of a human body. Thefe expreffions are apt to make us conceive God to be like ourfelves, as fome of the ancient heretics did. To correct fo abfurd a conceit, we muft compare thofe places with thofe

those of other texts, which tell us, that *God is a spirit,* and which upbraid the heathen for the abfurdnefs of their idolatry in reprefenting the infinite power and majefty of God by a material and fenfelefs image; thereby fuppofing God to be like the work of his own hands, and *changing his glory into the likenefs of a corruptible creature.* Thus the comparing thefe feveral texts together will convince us, that the places which mention the hands, or other parts of God Almighty, intend only to fet forth God's knowledge, power, and mercy by fuch fenfible reprefentations, as might make a deeper impreffion of his greatnefs and majefty upon our carnal minds and affections.

Lafly, The comparing one text with another is particularly ufeful for explaining the writings of the Prophets, efpecially thofe prophecies which relate to the times of the Gofpel. For example; when it is
fore-

foretold that *the mountain of the Lord's house should be established upon the top of the mountains, and all nations should flow unto it* [1] : Our Saviour gives the true interpretation of this prophecy, [m] when he tells the woman of *Samaria,* that *the hour cometh, when ye shall neither in this mountain* [*of* Samaria] *nor that at* Jerusalem, *worship the Father: But the true worshippers shall worship the Father in spirit and in truth*; that is, with a spiritual and reasonable service, without being confined in one certain country or place.

4. The last rule I shall offer for the explaining difficult places of Scripture, especially *such as relate to the outward government and ordinances of the Church,* is, that *we should have an especial regard to the practice and usage of the first and purest ages of the Church, and those*

---

[1] Isa. ii. 1.
[m] Joh. iv. 21, 23.

that

that were nearest the times of the Apostles.

This direction perhaps is not so proper for the use of unlearned persons; but if it had been observed by some that set up for teachers, it would have prevented several disputes that have very much disturbed the peace of the Church.

It is a received maxim, *that every law is best explained by the subsequent practice;* and if we apply this rule to the Christian law, it is certain that the primitive Christians had better advantages of knowing the mind of the Apostles, and the sense of their writings, meerly by living so near the apostolic age, than the greatest industry or learning can furnish us with, that live at this distance. And to suppose that the Christians who lived in those early days, would either carelessly lay aside, or wilfully deviate from the rules and orders which the Apostles gave to the Church by the direction of God's Spirit,

Spirit, is a great reflection upon the providence of God and his care of the Church, upon the honour of our holy religion, which, upon this fuppofition, could not maintain it's firſt conſtitution ſo long as moſt human polities have done, and upon the memory of thoſe glorious confeſſors and witneſſes to Chriſtianity, who planted the Goſpel with their preaching, and watered it with their blood, and on whoſe credit and teſtimony the authority of the Scripture-canon itſelf does very much depend.

So much reaſon is there for our paying a due deference to the judgment and practice of the primitive Church, in doubts relating to the writings and inſtitutions of the Apoſtles. And perhaps the only viſible means that is left to heal the breaches which diſtract the catholic Church, would be, if all parties were willing to refer their differences to the arbitration of the *four firſt ages.* At leaſt, if men would hear-

the HOLY SCRIPTURES. 89
hearken to the judgment of the earliest times of Chriſtianity, it would be a very proper means to put an end to ſome diſputes, which do very much diſturb our preſent age and Church, as will appear by inſtancing in a few particulars.

1. There have been, and ſtill are, ſeveral diſputes relating to original ſin, the nature of the goſpel covenant, and the means of entering into it, which would be in a great meaſure ſilenced, if men would but have a regard to the ſenſe and uſage of the primitive times; when the *baptizing of infants* was univerſally practiſed in all churches, as can be plainly proved by undeniable teſtimony. *Pelagius* and his followers, were the firſt that openly denied the doctrine of original ſin: And when they were urged with the argument taken from infant baptiſm, they could not deny but the practice of it was as old as Chriſtianity
it-

itself, [n] though the granting thus much did, in effect, overthrow the whole scheme of principles which they had advanced against the received doctrine of the catholic Church. The great esteem which the primitive Christians had for the sacrament of the Lord's supper, their looking upon it as the highest part of the christian worship, and never omitting the use of it upon their solemn days of devotion, sufficiently discovers what their opinion was concerning the death and sacrifice of Christ therein commemorated, and that they esteemed it to be the meritorious cause of their redemption. So that the *Socinians*, who deny the merit of Christ's death and sufferings, act very consistently with them-

---

[n] Cœlestii Pelagian. verba ap. Augustin. l. 2. contr. Pelag. & Cœlestium c. 5. *Infantes deberi baptizari in remissionem peccatorum, secundum regulam Universalis Ecclesiæ, & secundum Evangelii sententiam, confitemur.* Eadem fatentem *Pelagium* videre est, ibid. c. 17, 18.

selves in laying aside the use of this holy sacrament; but at the same time they confess that their doctrine, as well as their practice, in this particular, is a direct contradiction to the judgment of the universal Church in the best and purest ages.

2. Every one is sensible what eager disputes there are on foot about church-government, and how common it is to hear unlearned and ignorant people, who cannot possibly be judges of the merits of the cause, exclaim against the government of *Bishops* as antichristian, and the introducing of tyranny and ambition into the Church. To bring this controversy to a short issue, we only desire our adversaries would grant us these two things, which seem to be modest and reasonable requests. First, that the Scripture is at least as favourable to Episcopacy as to any other form of church-government, which they would set up in its room: (They that will not grant this, shew that
they

they never throughly ſtudied this controverſy.) And, ſecondly, that the ſenſe of the Scriptures, as to this point, may be decided by the judgment of the primitive Church, as the moſt competent witneſs of the practice of the Apoſtles. It is certain that ſeveral of thoſe who were the diſciples to the Apoſtles, ſuch as *Timothy, Titus, Ignatius, Polycarp, Clemens Romanus,* and *Dionyſius* the *Areopagite,* [a] &c. did exerciſe the epiſcopal office, the ſame for ſubſtance which is practiſed in our Church at this day; that is, they had in their ſingle capacity the chief care and overſight of many particular churches or congregations [b]: Not to inſiſt now, that St. *James,* one of the twelve Apoſtles, did plainly exerciſe the epiſcopal office, having his reſidence fixt at *Jeruſalem,* and preſiding over the elders and church there [c].

[a] V. *Euſeb.* Hiſt. Eccl. l. 3. c. 4. and l. 4. c. 23.
[b] *See this fully proved in* Dr. Maurice's defence of Dioceſan Epiſcopacy.
[c] *See* Acts xxi. 18. xii. 17. xv. 13.

It

It is as evident that there could be no room for ambition, or secular interest in these early times, when all the bishopricks brought along with them was a nearer step to sufferings and martyrdom. It is no less certain, that this form of government was universally settled over the whole Christian Church in the age immediately succeeding the times of the Apostles. The adversaries of Episcopacy have been often challenged to produce one single example of any Church settled without Bishops, for the space of above fifteen hundred years after Christ; and they have not yet been able to give any instance to the contrary, that could satisfy any person of ordinary learning or judgment.

Now after such pregnant proofs of the antiquity of the episcopal government, for men still to cry out upon it as a remnant of Popery, is to make Popery much older than it really is, and thereby give greater advantage to its cause, than it becomes those men to do who profess themselves to be such

such zealous Protestants. For if it is once yielded that Popery was settled in the times next to the apostolic age, it will be no hard matter for the emissaries of that Church to persuade people, that what we call Popery is really the true and primitive state of Christianity. Such advantage does a *rash and ignorant zeal against Popery* afford to that very cause, which it seems with so much vehemence to oppose. And as a great master of controversy hath observed, [d] " Those who forego the testimony " of antiquity, as all opposers of the " Church of *England* must do, must " unavoidably run into insuperable " difficulties in dealing with the Pa- " pists, which the principles of our " Church do lead us through," whose glory and happiness it is to have been reformed by the rule of God's word, and the pattern of the best and purest ages: Upon which account it is so much envied and maligned by

[d] *Bishop* Stillingfleet, *Preface to the Unreasonableness of Separation*, p. 5.

the

the popish party, who, not without reason, look upon it as the most formidable enemy that they have, because it confutes their false pretences to antiquity upon the surest principles.

The inference I shall make from what has been said concerning the obscurity of several Scripture passages, is this, That we ought to read the Scriptures with an humble, modest, and teachable disposition * with a willingness to embrace all truths which are plainly delivered there, how contrary soever to our own former opinions or prejudices: That we ought in matters of difficulty readily hearken to the judgment of our teachers, and those that are set over us in the Lord: That we should check every presumptuous *thought or reasoning* ᶠ *which exalts itself* against any of those mysterious truths therein revealed, still remembring that *God is great, and we know him not* ᵍ, and

---

* *Omnis scriptura sacra eo spiritu debet legi quo scripta est.* Kempis Imit. Christi, l. 1. c. 5.
ᶠ Λογισμὸς, 2 Cor. x. 5.   ᵍ Job xxxvi. 26.

it is impossible, for us *to search out the Almighty unto perfection* [h]. And if we thus search after the truth *in the love of it* [i] we shall not miss of finding that knowledge which will make us wise unto salvation.

CHAP. IV.

Concerning the Historical books of the old Testament, *and what things are chiefly observable in our reading of them.*

Hitherto I have offered only some general considerations, which tend to the illustrating the stile of the holy Scriptures, and justifying that method which the holy Spirit hath pitched upon for instructing us in all saving truths, and taking off those prejudices which hinder many from the careful reading and study of the holy Scriptures. I shall now proceed to give more particular directions con-

[h] Job xi. 7.   [i] 2 Thes. ii. 10.

cerning

the HOLY SCRIPTURES. 97

cerning the ufe we are to make of the feveral parts of the holy writings. And becaufe I do not intend to treat of every book by itfelf, I fhall confider them under fome general heads, to which they may conveniently be reduced.

And to begin with the *old Teftament*, we may divide the books of it into thefe four forts; the *Hiftorical*, the *Moral*, the *Pfalms*, and the *Prophets*. I fhall make fome obfervations upon each of thefe general heads, which may help to explain the chief intent and defign of thofe feveral writings, and the principal ufes we are to make of them.

The firft that come under our confideration are the hiftorical books.

Reading of hiftory is commonly reckoned one of the moft diverting ftudies we can entertain ourfelves with, in which refpect the Scripture hiftory has incomparably the advan-
E tage

tage above all other writings in that kind, inasmuch as it contains the most ancient records that are extant in the world, and relates the most remarkable occurrences that ever happened in it. The *Bible* gives us an account of the beginning of the world, and affords us a prospect unto the end of it. It begins with the history of the creation, of the state of innocence, of the deluge, and of the peopling the world afterwards: Of all which wonderful transactions the heathens had only an obscure tradition; a tradition indeed so universally spread, as doth sufficiently attest the truth of the Scripture records, as to each of these particulars; but withal so mixt and darkened with fabulous circumstances, as very much weakened the credit of the whole relation. So that those who could not have recourse to a more authentic account of these important affairs, were in doubt whether the world had any beginning or not, and from thence came to question the being of its author.

The

The sacred history gives likewise an account of the fall of man, of the entrance of sin into the world, and those many evils and calamities which it brought along with it. This the wisest Philosophers were very much puzzled to trace the original of, or give a satisfactory reason, how so much evil should come into a world that was made by a good God. But the Scripture account displays both the justice and goodness of God in this matter, because it discovers to us, that God took occasion from thence to make known the riches of his mercy toward the lost sons of *Adam*, by sending his own Son into the world to redeem them, that *where sin had abounded, grace might much more abound* [k]. Here we see the scene of man's redemption beginning to open immediately after the creation, to shew us that *Christ was the end of the law* [l], and of all the dispensations of Providence which preceded it; that *he* [m]

[k] Rom. v. 2o.   [l] Rom. x. 4.   [m] Rev. xiii. 8.

was *the Lamb slain* in the purpose and decree of God, *before the foundation of the world,* and promised ἀπὸ χρόνων αἰωνίων *from or before ancient times* [n], though for great and wise reasons *he did not appear till towards the* [o] *conclusion of the ages of the world.* So we find one and the same design pursued from one end of the *Bible* to the other, and all the sacred writers agree in displaying the *great mystery of godliness* by various steps and degrees, from the promise of the blessed *seed* in Paradise [p], to the end and consummation of all things.

I am sensible that there are great difficulties to be met with in the three first chapters of *Genesis,* which have made some ancient writers question whether all the particulars therein related were to be understood literally or not: And of late an opinion has much prevailed, which maintains that

[n] Tit. i. 2. *confer* LXX. *Interp. ad* Psal. lxxvii. 5. Isai. lxiii. 9, 11.
[o] Ἐπὶ συντελείᾳ τῶν αἰώνων, Heb. ix. 26. [p] Gen. iii. 15.

Moses

the HOLY SCRIPTURES.

Moses *wrote this part of his history as a law-giver, and not as a philosopher.*

If the meaning of this expression be, that *Moses* did not write with that accuracy of phrase, or with those terms of art which *Des Cartes* or *Galilæo* would have done upon the same subject, it is readily granted; for such a discourse would have been above the apprehension of common understandings, and so not answered the intent of *Moses*'s writing. I think we may, without derogation to the Scripture authority, own that the Philosophy of it is popular, and suited to the apprehensions of the unlearned: Of which kind we may allow those Scripture expressions to be, which suppose the *sun to move,* and the *earth to stand still*; and I cannot see why we should lay such a stress upon them, as out of deference to their authority, to check any philosophical enquiries which may favour the contrary opinion; since the great asserters of the earth's motion would in a popular discourse comply with the common way of speaking.

But when this pretence is carried so far, as to explode the history of the *six days creation*, delivered with such particular circumstances by *Moses*, and those confirmed by the rest of the sacred writers, and to reject his whole narrative as a piece of pure invention, because it does not agree with an *hypothesis*, where I think it is plain, that invention has a very great share; and where the difficulties that may be objected, will be found to be greater: Such an undertaking betrays the over-fondness ingenious men are apt to have for their own schemes, and the little regard they pay to Scripture authority, when it stands in competition with a beloved notion.

I would not be thought to undervalue Philosophy, which is certainly a noble and useful study, as it searches out the wisdom of God in his works. But I think it may find employment enough, without entering into that nice and uncertain speculation, how God made the world, which a modern
Phi-

Philosopher of some-note has looked upon as an undertaking above the reach of human understanding q; which may very well content itself, with enquiring by what laws nature works ever since its settlement at the creation, and not presume to confine God almighty to the same rules in creating the world, which inferior agents are tied to follow in continuing it. For we may observe, that even in the ordinary course of generation, the first vital functions are not performed in the same manner before the formation of the heart, liver, and brain, as they are when the *fœtus* is brought to perfection. And granting this difference between God's works whilst they were making, and after they were made, and the course of nature settled, I doubt not but *Moses*'s history of the creation will deserve that character, which one that was an eminent Philosopher, as well as a

---

q *Majus est mundus opus, quam ut assequi mens humana ejus molitionem possit.* Gassend. Physic.

good

good Divine [c] gives of it, *viz. That it is such a plain, brief, and unaffected account of the creation, as must needs recommend itself to the belief of all impartial men.*

Especially if we add this consideration to the former, *viz.* That *Moses*'s principal design in writing this history of the six days creation, was to give a plain intelligible account of the visible part of it [d], or of this planetary system, which has the sun for it's center, as our excellent expositor Bishop *Patrick* speaks, in order to the confuting that sort of idolatry, which chiefly prevailed in his time, and consisted in giving worship to the heavenly bodies, or some principal parts of the lower world.

These two considerations will, I presume, afford a sufficient answer to the philosophical objections which are commonly urged against the

[c] *Bp.* Wilkins *of Nat. Relig.* p. 65.
[d] *V.* Cyril. *l.* 2. *cont.* Julian. *p.* 50. &c. *Edit.* Spanhem.

Scripture hiſtory of the creation. But becauſe *ſome modern hypotheſes*, whatever reputation they may have procured to their authors, yet have manifeſtly tended to weaken the credit of *Moſes*'s account of the primæval ſtate of the world, it may not be amiſs briefly to vindicate the authority of this firſt, and as I may juſtly call it, fundamental part of Scripture revelation, by pointing out the moſt remarkable ſtrokes of divine wiſdom, which are ſo conſpicuous in this narrative, that ſome of them have been honourably mentioned, even by heathens themſelves.

And the firſt remarkable paſſage I ſhall take notice of is, that *Moſes* aſcribes the creation of the world wholly to the free pleaſure of God, and aſſigns no other cauſe of it, but the divine decree, which he expreſſes by God's pronouncing the [e]

[e] Gen. i. 3.

Fiat

Fiat within himself. Now this is so worthy a conception of the almightiness of the divine will, that *Longinus* [f], who looked upon *Moses* only as a wise law-giver, not as an inspired writer, pitches upon this expression as an instance of the true *sublime*, as having a grandeur in it suitable to the majesty of the person whom he represents, and such as conveys to our minds a just idea of God's omnipotence. The truth here asserted ought the more to be regarded, because it was above the reach of some of the wisest philosophers, who thought that God's goodness could not lie idle and not exert itself; and from thence inferred, that since God was good from all eternity, the world must be co-eternal with him. Whereas reason itself, rightly informed, instructs us, that though God be essentially good, yet as he is, or can be, a debtor to none, so the emanations of his goodness must be free and unconstrained, and consequently

[f] Περὶ ὕψους Sect. 7.

the

the exercise of it must be limited by such measures as seem best to his infinite wisdom. And this doctrine, which is so clearly deducible from the place before us, is expresly delivered in that heavenly hymn, recorded in the *revelation* [g], *thou hast created all things, and for thy pleasure they are and were created.*

The next remarkable passage, which I shall recommend to the devout reader's observation, is, that *rest* which *Moses* [h] informs us God enjoyed, when he had finished his works of creation. And I the rather insist upon this passage, because it is mentioned with approbation by that eminent Philosopher my Lord *Bacon* [i], and therefore I hope his judgment may screen it from the censure of being a *popular and unphilosophical notion.* For we are not to understand by it, such a rest as poor mortals are refreshed with after

[g] Ch. iv. 11. [h] Gen. ii. 2. [i] *Preface to* Instaur. magna, & alibi.

their being wearied with hard labour, but that pleasure which the Almighty took in viewing his works, and pronouncing them to be *exceeding good*, which the *Psalmist* calls the *Lord's rejoicing in his works* [k]. Whereas in all *that sore travel which God gives to the sons of men to be exercised therewith*, they can take no lasting rest nor comfort, but find all of them to end in *vanity and vexation of spirit*.

It is likewise agreed by the unanimous consent of all interpreters, both *Jewish* and *Christian*, that the *Sabbath*, a feast of God's own immediate institution, was designed to typify and represent that *heavenly rest which remains for the people of God* [l] after this world is ended, when they shall cease from the labours and troubles of life, see God and contemplate his works with the greatest pleasure and delight, and also take a view of their own

[k] Psal. civ. 31.   [l] Heb. iv. 9.

good

the HOLY SCRIPTURES. 109

good works with comfort and satisfaction; for the Scripture tells us [m], that they will also *follow us,* or *go along with us* [n] into that state of bliss.

The same consent of antiquity will justify us in assigning this as one reason, why God thought fit to divide the creation into six days work; *viz.* to pre-signify that this world should last six millennaries of years, (according to that maxim of Scripture [o], That one day is with the Lord as a thousand years) and then the Sabbath, or *millennium* of rest, should follow.

However that be, the arguments which learned men [p] have brought to prove that the Sabbath was observed by the patriarchs from the very creation, and that the fourth commandment, and the preceding institution mentioned, *Exod.* xvi. 23.

---

[m] Rev. xiv. 13. [n] Ἀκολυθεῖ μετ' αὐτῶν. Comp. Luke ix. 49. [o] 2 Pet. iii 8.

[p] *See Bishop* Usher's *Epist.* 205. *and Dr.* Allix's *Reflections upon* Genesis, *Chap.* vii.

was

was only a revival of that primitive usage which had been intermitted during the *Egyptian* bondage; as also that custom which has generally prevailed among all nations, of reckoning their time by a septenary revolution of days [q]. All these arguments, I say, are a very good proof that *Moses*'s account of the six days work of creation is literally true.

A third particular that deserves our notice in the Scripture history of the creation, is the account which *Moses* gives us of the nature and origin of the soul, *viz.* that is was not made out of matter, but immediately created by God, and breathed into the body which was formed out of dust; that it is the *breath of life*, which gives life, sense, and motion to the body: Nay, that it has a principle of true divine life in

[q] *V.* Theophil. *ad* Autolycum. l. 2. p. 95. *Edit.* Oxon, & Grotii *notas ad* l. c. 16. *de Veritat. Chr. Relig.*

itself,

itself, *being made after the image and likeness of God,* the intellectual perfections of human understanding and will, bearing the nearest resemblance to the divine nature of any powers we can discover in this lower part of the creation. From whence it follows, that the soul has a happiness of it's own, independant of the body, and consequently is capable of a divine and heavenly state. I hope this may pass for a strain above vulgar notions, and gives as good an account of the dignity and prerogatives of human souls, as the acutest philosophers can furnish us with.

Fourthly, *Moses* makes the institution of marriage co-equal with the creation, and confines it to one man and one woman, or at least represents this as the most perfect and primitive pattern of that state; which is such a wise and just restraint of mens appetites as the laws

laws or manners of few nations before the times of Christianity did countenance. Hereby we are instructed likewise that the state of matrimony is the ordinance of God, and not only the prudent institution of human law-givers, as the heathens generally thought it to be.

I have already observed that *Moses* gives us a better account of man's fall, than the wisest of the heathens could attain to, though they reasonably concluded from the unruliness of mens passions, and the want of sufficient power in the mind to check and controul them, that there was a lapse, or weakning, of the higher powers of the soul [q], whereby it had lost that dominion which it originally had over the whole man: So that the Scripture history of this matter ought to be valued, if it were only for this

---

[q] Homo non ut a matre, sed ut a noverca natura editus est in vitam —— animo anxio ad molestias, humili ad timores, molli ad labores, prono ad libidines, in quo tamen inest tanquam obrutus quidam divinus ignis ingenii & mentis. *Cicero apud Augustin. l. 4. contr. Julianum.*

reason, that it is the only account that hath been tranſmitted to us of that univerſal corruption which has overſpread the world, and which all men have reaſon to be ſenſible of, and to lament. Thus much may be ſaid in general for the juſtification of that part of the *Moſaic* hiſtory; and if we proceed to examine the ſeveral circumſtances of this ſtory, we may obſerve that *Moſes* has in a very lively manner deſcribed the paſſions and weak ſide of human nature, in the account he gives us of the fall.

Firſt, He gives us to underſtand, that the tempter infuſed into *Eve* a diſlike of her own condition, and an aiming at a happineſs above it: Accordingly experience juſtifies the truth of this obſervation, *that pride goes before a fall*; and ambition and diſcontent are the uſual inlets to ruin and miſery.

The lovely aſpect of the forbidden fruit does admoniſh us, that preſent temptations work more powerfully upon our ſenſes and affections, than

dry

dry thinking and reasoning can do upon our judgments.

As soon as our parents had eaten the forbidden fruit, the text tells us, that '*the eyes of them both were opened;* implying, that their eyes were opened in a different sense from that which the tempter had insinuated to them, ' namely, to apprehend clearly the evil they had done, and the misery they had brought upon themselves, thereby instructing us in this great and useful truth, that however sin may blind the eyes while we are in the eager pursuit of it, yet when it is once finished and the pleasure over, the mask is taken off, and it appears in its true colours; the mind is awakened to a thorough sense of the greatness of the crime, and her own folly in committing it. *Perfecto demum scelere, magnitudo ejus intellecta est*, as that accurate describer of human nature, *Tacitus*‘, represents it.

* Gen. iii. 7.   * Ibid. viii. 5.   ‘ *Annal.* lib. xiv.

the HOLY SCRIPTURES. 115

Their *hiding themselves among the trees of the garden* ᶜ is a lively reprefentation of cowardlinefs of guilt, and that the *noife of a fhaken leaf* is enough to fright thofe that are confcious to themfelves that they deferve punifhment.

Having mentioned this circumftance, I fhall venture to digrefs a little for the explaining the true meaning of the whole verfe where it is mentioned, becaufe I find great exception taken againft the literal fenfe of the former part of it, where it is faid, that our firft parents *heard the voice of the Lord God walking in the garden in the cool of the day*, as if it were a very improper reprefentation of the divine nature. But furely that learned perfon who makes this objection, is too well acquainted with antiquity, to be ignorant, that it was the unanimous fenfe of the ancient Church, both ᵈ *Jewifh*

ᶜ Gen. iii. 8.
ᵈ *See* Dr. Allix's *Judgment of the* Jewifh *Church againft the* Unitarians, *efpecially* c. 13, 14, 15.

and

and *Christian* [e], that as God made the world by his Son, all the dispensations of providence, especially the affairs of the Church, were ordered and disposed by him. This opinion is built upon those texts of Scripture, where the incommunicable name of *Jehovah* is given to an angel [f] and cannot be reasonably understood of any other but the Son of God, who is expressly called *the angel of the covenant*, by the prophet *Malachi* [g]: This second person of the blessed Trinity, as he sometimes took upon him the character of an angel, so at other times he assumed an human shape, as an emblem, or earnest, of the incarnation. Thus he appeared to *Abra-*

---

[e] *See the Proofs, both from the* New Testament, *and the Primitive Fathers, in Bishop* Bull's Defens. Fid. Nic. c. 1. §. 1.

[f] *See* Gen. xxii. 11, 12, 15, 16, 18. ch. xxxi. 11, 13. Exod. iii. 2, 4, 6. ch. xxiii. 20, 21. *comp. with* Exod. xxxiii. 2, 3, 14. *and with* ch. xiii. 21. *and* ch. xiv. 19.

[g] Malachi iii. 1.

ham [h], to *Jacob* [i], to *Joshua* [k], to *Gideon* [l]; and it is altogether as probable he might converse with our first parents under the same shape in paradise, as it is particularly affirmed by *Theophilus Antiochenus* [m]; and those expressions, *let us make man*, and *Adam is become like one of us*, plainly imply a plurality of divine persons concerned in these transactions, and were always interpreted to that sense by the antient writers, both *Jews* and *Christians*. And as for the expression of God's *walking in the wind, or cool of the day*, it is a manifest allusion to the time of walking in those hot countries, which was usually toward the evening.

But if this sense of the words be not accepted, they are fairly capable of another, by joining the participle [walking] with the substantive [voice]

[h] Gen. xviii. 2, 13, 17, 22, 26. [i] Gen. xxxii. 24. [k] Josh. v. 13, 14, 15. [l] Judg. vi. 11, 14, 16, 21. [m] Lib. 2. *ad* Autolycum. p. 129. *Ed.* Oxon.

and

and tranflating the word thus, *they heard the voice of the Lord God difperfing itfelf*, (fo the phrafe is ufed *Jerem.* xlvi. 22.) or *waxing loud, or increafing among the trees of the garden*. Thus the word תהלך fignifies, when it is joined with קול *Exod.* xix. 19, and then the fenfe will be, that the divine *Schechinah* appeared with a terrible found accompanying it as a token of God's difpleafure. A ftill voice is fometimes mentioned in Scripture [n] as a mark of God's prefence; and the very apprehenfion of his appearing is enough to put guilty perfons in a great confternation; but a ftormy wind and tempeft is the token of his coming with anger and vengeance [o]. And taking the words in either of thefe fenfes, the context seems to favour the expofition; for when God called *Adam*, in the following verfe, he replies, *I heard thy voice in the garden, and was afraid.*

[n] *See* 2 Sam. v. 24. 1 Kings xix. 12.
[o] *See* Pfal. xviii. 10, 14. Ifa. xxx. 30. Ezek. xiii. 13.

I am

the HOLY SCRIPTURES. 119

I am fenfible that there are feveral difficulties relating to the *three firſt chapters of Geneſis*, which ſtill want to be placed in a better light; and in order to the clearing them, we muſt acknowledge, that fometimes a myſtical and ſpiritual fenſe is hidden under a literal one: That by the *Serpent* we are to underſtand the *Devil*, making uſe of the *Serpent* as his inſtrument, is confirmed by the unanimous expoſition of the ſacred writers themſelves, and thoſe both of the *old* and *new Teſtament* ⁱ. Nor indeed was it congruous that *Moſes*, who had taken notice only of the viſible creation, ſhould preſently introduce angels or ſpirits into this lower world. In like manner by the *nakedneſs*, at the difcovery of which our firſt parents were confounded immediately upon their fall, we are not only to underſtand the nakedneſs of the body, but likewiſe their minds being di-

---

ⁱ Iſa. xxvii. 1. Luke x. 19. John viii. 44. Rev. xii. 9. xx. 2.

vested of it's natural ornaments of purity and innocence [r]. By that *strict guard* which is kept about the tree of life, we are to understand that eternal life is a happiness out of our reach, and from which we must be totally excluded, unless Christ *gives us* power *to eat of the tree of life, which is in the midst of the paradise of God,* which he has promised to do to his faithful servants [s].

I shall leave the further pursuit of this argument to those that have understanding in the depths of the holy oracles, who in this, as well as in many other parts of the Scriptures, will discover several important truths to be couched under such expressions, as a careless and unattentive reader would take little or no notice of, and shall only just observe, that two of the principal difficulties relating to this place, *viz.* concerning the *situation of paradise,* and why the tempter discoursed with *Eve*

---

[r] *Compare* Exod. xxxii. 25. Rev. iii. 18. xvi. 15. 2 Cor. v. 3. [s] Rev. ii. 7.

under the shape of a *Serpent*, have been happily cleared by two learned critics of our own age; the one by Monsieur *Huet*, in his accurate treatise, *de Paradiso*; the other by his present *Grace of Canterbury*, in his learned discourse of *Idolatry* [a], who observes that the *Hebrew* word *Saraph*, which signifies a *fiery Serpent* [b], in the plural *Seraphim*, denotes likewise an *order of angels with wings* [c], who, by the clearness and brightness, of their aspect, appear as it were flaming and fiery. From whence this most reverend author ingeniously conjectures that the Devil appeared in the form of such a fiery Serpent, as resembled a flaming angel, and so was mistaken by *Eve* for one of those bright *Seraphims*, which made up part of the *Schechinah* of the *Logos*; and from the same grounds assigns the reason why Serpents were esteemed sacred and

[a] P. 356. [b] Numb. xxi. 6. Deut. viii. 15. Isa. xiv. 19. [c] Isa. vi. 2, 6.

worship-

worshipped in several parts of the *Heathen* world.

My chief design being to illustrate the sense, and assert the authority of Holy Scripture, I thought it would be no improper digression, if I spent some time in clearing the sense of this important portion of Holy Writ, and vindicating it from some objections, which have been of late industriously revived against its credit and authority. And I hope, that what has been said, may be in some measure serviceable to satisfy mens doubts in this point, and to preserve a due reverence for this most primitive part of the antiquities of the world, and upon the truth of which the authority of *both Testaments* doth very much depend.

Another particular relating to the books of *Moses*, which I would recommend to the observation of the attentive reader, is this, that in his writings, and indeed throughout the *old Testament*, we may observe

two

the HOLY SCRIPTURES. 123

two different systems or schemes of religion ᵈ if I may so term them, the one of the patriarchs, prophets, and eminent persons among the *Jews*; the other more adapted to the temper of the more ignorant and inferior sort, and most regarded by those who lived in the corrupt and degenerate times of the *Jewish* state.

The former is an institution purely spiritual, and built upon the foundations of natural religion, (whose principles are there placed in their truest and best light) especially upon these two fundamental principles of it, the love of God above all things, of our neighbour as ourselves ᵉ. It enjoins men to *do justly, to love mercy, and to walk humbly with God* ᶠ: To live under a grateful sense of God's providence, and a comfortable hope of obtaining his promises, especially that great one concerning the Messias, and all those heavenly

---

ᵈ *See* Euseb. præparat. Evang. lib. 7. c. 6, 7, &c.
ᵉ *See* Mark xii. 28, &c.   ᶠ Mich. vi. 8.

F 2   bles-

blessings of which he was to be the author. The law taken in this sense, St. *Paul* calls *spiritual* and *holy, and just and good* [g], and those Jews that practised it, he calls Jews *inwardly, whose circumcision was that of the heart, in the spirit, and not in the letter.* Rom. ii. and with a regard to this more perfect part of the *Mosaical* dispensation, he often insists upon these points, that the Fathers, *Abel, Enoch, Noah,* and *Abraham, were justified by faith, as well as we Christians* [h], that all the faithful, both before and under the law, *eat the same spiritual meat, drank the same spiritual drink* [i], and *embraced the same heavenly promises* [k], which are now more explicitly revealed by the Gospel.

The other system of religion consisted merely in outward observances, either such as related to the public worship of God in the tabernacle, or concerned mens private be-

---

[g] Rom. vii. 12, 14. [h] Heb. xi. 2, &c. Rom. iv. 13. Gal. iii. 8, 17, 18. [i] 1 Cor. x. 3, 4. [k] Heb. xi. 13.

haviour

haviour in the ordinary way of life. And these the same Apostle [f] stiles *weak and beggarly elements.*

The former of these none can deny to be worthy of God; for it lays down a much more perfect scheme of religion than the wisest *Heathens* could ever discover by the dim light of corrupt nature; and it is often taken notice of by the antient Fathers [g], and the other learned advocates for Christianity [h], that the best notions the Philosophers and Heathen Legislators had about religious matters were drawn from the writings of the *old Testament.*

But the other part of the *Mosaical* system, consisting chiefly of external rites and ordinances, hath been thought by *Infidels* a considerable objection against the divine authority of the law

---

[f] Gal. iv. 9.
[g] *Vid.* Justin. M. Apol. II. (Verius I.) *n.* 76, 77. Edit. Oxon. Clem. Alex. Strom. *l.* 1. *p.* 302. *l.* 2. *p.* 394. *l.* 5. *p.* 391. Euseb. Præp. Evan. *l.* 9. *c.* 3. *l.* 13. *c.* 7. & alibi passim.
[h] Huetii Demonstr. Evang. Prop. 4. *c.* 2. *n.* 14, &c. 11, per totum.

of *Moses*, as containing in it such unaccountable injunctions, as they think unworthy of the wisdom of God.

But the force of this objection will be taken off by these two considerations. 1. That some of the *Jewish* laws and ordinances which seem strange to us, had a particular respect to the rights and religious customs of the neighbouring nations, as has been fully proved by learned men [o], and is confessed by that learned *Jew Maimonides* [p]: God intending to preserve the *Jews* from falling into the idolatries of the *Heathen*, partly by retaining in their laws some indifferent customs of theirs, innocently introduced; and partly, by instituting other ceremonies in opposition to the cruel, impure, and absurd rites, which the *Pagans* used in the worship of their idols. 2. That several precepts of the ceremonial law have a *moral sense* couched under them, it being the ancient way of instructing men

---

[o] See particularly Dr. Spencer de Legib. Hebr.
[p] More Nevoch. par. 3. c. 29. & sequent.

the HOLY SCRIPTURES. 127

by outward figns and fymbolical reprefentations, as appears by the famous *Symbols* of *Pythagoras:* A method of inftruction which he probably learnt from the *Eaftern* Sages, with whom he had converfed [d]. To this fenfe, *Jofephus* expounds [e] many precepts of the ceremonial law, and feveral places of the [f] *new Teftament* do plainly favour fuch an interpretation. And the precept of circumcifion is expounded to a moral fenfe by *Mofes* himfelf, *Deut.* x. 16. 3. That a great part of the rites enjoined in the fervice of God by the ordinances of the law, were a *figure or parable for the time then prefent* [g], did typify and exhibit in myftical reprefentations the days of the Meffias, as the Apoftles have fully proved in their writings, particularly St. *Paul* in the Epiftle to the *Hebrews*, the *Jews* themfelves of thofe times agreeing

[d] *See* Prov. i. 6. [e] *Antiq. l.* 4. [f] *See* Acts x. 14, 15, 28. 1 Cor. v. 6, 7. *and* ch. ix. 9.
[g] Παραβολὴ εἰς τὸν καιρὸν τὸν ἐνεστῶτα. Heb. ix. 9.

with them in the same notions [d], as several of the more modern *Jews* have done since. Indeed without supposing the ceremonial law to be a figure of the Gospel, it is as hard to reconcile these two schemes of the *Jewish* religion with each other, as with the Gospel itself. Whereas if we compare the [e] rudiments of the law with the more perfect revelation of the Gospel, and explain them by the light which that lets in upon them, we presently see the *veil taken away from the face of* Moses, and are able to *look to the end* or principal design of *that* institution, *which* though ordained by God himself, *was to be abolished*, and give place unto a better. So that this very objection affords us a new proof of the divine original of the holy Scriptures, because it helps to discover the harmony and connexion of the several parts of those divine writings.

The next remarkable passage relating to the books of *Moses*, which

[d] *See* Philo's *Writings*. [e] Στοιχεῖα, Gal. iv. 9.

I would

I would desire the attentive reader to take particular notice of, is, God's chusing *Abraham* and his seed, separating them from the rest of the world, and making a covenant with them, that he would be their God, and they should be his people; and that in the fulness of time the promised seed should arise out of that nation. This was the first great step that God made towards the fulfilling the promise of the Messias: In order to the making which promise good, it was fit that God should make choice of some particular family, or people, from whence he should descend, or else he must have sprung from idolaters, which would have been by no means suitable to the dignity of his person, or the design of his coming. Accordingly the people from whence he was to derive his original, was separated from all the rest of the world by a peculiar set of rites and ordinances, which made them nicely scrupulous of conversing or mixing with other nations. It was

like-

likewise convenient, that Christ should not come into the world without some necessary preparations, in order to his due reception there. Thereupon God sanctified a people on purpose, among whom Christ should be born, and raised up a succession of prophets among them who foretold all the circumstances relating to his appearance, from whose writings a certain description might be given of him, whenever he should appear.

If so great a person had of a sudden appeared in the world without any notice given of his coming, the unexpectedness of so extraordinary a blessing might have caused wonder and surprise; but it would not have been reckoned an effect of *God's determinate counsel and fore-knowledge*, and of that πολυποίκιλΘ- σοφία *that manifold wisdom* [b], which by various steps and degrees carried on this design for the space of four thousand years together, before it was fully compleat and brought to perfection. But when the

[b] Eph. iii. 10.

Messias was ushered into the world with so much previous pomp and solemnity, that 'was a sensible demonstration that this *great mystery of godliness, God manifest in the flesh*, was the master-piece of the divine wisdom, and that all the lesser dispensations of providence were subservient to this great end.

This variety of prophecies which prepared the way for the coming of the Messias, doth likewise afford a satisfactory answer to that objection, which worldly-minded men are apt to suggest against the obscurity of Christ's birth and manner of living. They think it strange, that the Saviour of mankind should be born, and live obscurely in a corner; that he that is described *as the desire of all nations* [c], must be sought for in *Palestine*, an inconsiderable spot of ground, and in *Galilee*, the most despicable part of that country.

In reply to which objection, I shall not now insist upon the answer which St. *Paul* [d] gives to it, that God's power

[c] Hag. ii. 7. [d] 1 Cor. i. 27.

doth then most eminently appear, when *he chuses the weak* and contemptible *things of the world to confound the things that are mighty.* It is a sufficient reply to say, that the many prophecies of the *old Testament*, which gave a character of the Messias from his cradle to his grave, render him as easily discoverable, as if he had spent his whole life in the most public place in the world; and like the Star which appeared at his birth, give a sufficient direction to those that were at the greatest distance where to find him. If such a person was to come into the world, he must necessarily make his first appearance in some particular place or country; and surely no nation so fit for that purpose, as that which had the custody of those oracles which foretold the most remarkable circumstances of his life and actions.

The observations I have hitherto made, do chiefly relate to the account the Scripture gives of those two remarkable occurrences, the *creation of the world*, and the *promise of the Messias*.

Messias. These are the two *pillars*, or *boundaries of providence*, if I may so speak, and all the wheels and movements of it are confined within this sphere. The holy writers call them by the name of the *old and new creation*; and by their assistance we can take an intire view of both worlds, that which we now live in, and the other which we expect hereafter. And this certainly ought to recommend the sacred writings to the perusal of all those, who have the curiosity either of searching out the original of things, or of prying into their end and conclusion.

Before I leave this head, I shall make one general remark concerning the remaining parts of the *old Testament* history, namely, That there we find the history of this nation exactly pursued, and in a natural series of events for the space of near one thousand five hundred years, the principal transactions having such a connexion with, and dependence upon, each other, that they do mutually support

and

and confirm one another's credit, as hath been already obferved [e]. During all which time we may take notice that this people were fure to be happy or miferable, according as they kept clofe to, or departed from, the worfhip of the true God, and the obfervance of that law which he had given them. Which circumftance is not only a remarkable inftance of God's overruling providence, but likewife a fignal verification of thofe promifes and threatnings which God had made the fanction of his laws and ordinances.

I fhall clofe up my remarks upon this head, with this obfervation, that the main body of the facred hiftory, and all the chief materials of it, are taken out of the public records and monuments of the nation, to which the writers themfelves do often appeal, particularly in the books of *Kings* and *Chronicles*. The connexion which is obfervable between the feveral books of the Scripture hiftory, is likewife a plain indication, that they

[e] Chap. ii.

were digested by public authority, and not the product of private pens. Which one thing is a pregnant proof of the divine authority of the sacred writings, to any one that considers that all the pious princes and magistrates among the *Jews* undertook nothing of moment without advice and direction from God, who raised up a a succession of prophets among them for that very purpose. In this respect the compilers of the *Jewish* history have very much the advantage, in point of credit, of the historians of most other nations, especially of the *Greek* historians, as *Josephus* [s] observes; inasmuch as the *Greek* writers were neither appointed by authority to preserve the memory of former transactions, nor compiled their writings out of public or antient records, and were more ambitious of shewing their wit and eloquence, and telling their story in an elegant and plausible stile, than of transmitting a faithful account of

[s] Lib. 1. *cont. Appian. initio.*

mat-

matters of fact to posterity. Whereas the holy writers discover nothing of vanity or ostentation, of partiality or corrupt affection, but write with a a native simplicity, and unaffected air of sincerity, without flattery or prejudice, neither concealing their own private infirmities, nor palliating the vices or miscarriages of their greatest princes, but delivering their thoughts with great freedom, and speaking the truth without reserve: As if their only design was to give God the glory, and recommend their writings to the good opinion of their readers by a naked manifestation of the truth, which, when it is delivered plainly and without disguise, commands an assent, and works more powerfully upon the mind, than all the art in the world.

CHAP. V.

Concerning the Moral Writings of the Old Testament.

THE books of the *old Testament* that come next under our confideration, are the *moral writings* properly fo called, that is, fuch whofe chief defign is to inftruct us in the ways of virtue, and give rules for the direction and good government of our lives. Such are the books of *Job*, the *Proverbs* and *Ecclefiaftes*.

The book of *Job* was written on purpofe to teach us the great duty of patience and fubmiffion to God's will in all events: A duty, which it powerfully recommends to us, both by the example of that holy perfon who was fo eminent an inftance of *fuffering affliction and of patience*; and alfo by many arguments taken from the confideration of the greatnefs of God's majefty, with

with whom it is high prefumption for poor mortals to contend; of his infinite purity and holinefs, *in whofe fight* the beft men *cannot be juftified, if God will enter into* ftrict *judgment with them:* And, laftly, from the unfearchablenefs of his judgments, which are always true and righteous, though we cannot always comprehend the reafons of them. And I doubt not but pious and devout fouls may find great pleafure, as well as reap much profit by the careful perufal of this book; which recommends itfelf to the reader above all other books of holy Writ, by the wit and elegancy of the compofure, where human paffions are defcribed with the moft tender and lively ftrokes, where are to be found the moft elevated and noble thoughts concerning the power and majefty of God, and the moft devout expreffions of that fubmiffion and refignation which is due to his will, and of that truft and

and confidence which good men have in his mercy, even in the depth of their afflictions, arising from the testimony of their conscience and the sense of their own integrity. And these pious meditations are clothed in such natural and easy words, as convey to our minds a just idea of *natural Religion* when it was in its prime, and as it was practised in those early ages, before the tradition of the creation and of the flood was lost, or the world quite over-run with idolatry.

The *Proverbs*, as they were written by *Solomon*, a Prince famous in all ages for his wisdom and experience, so they contain excellent instructions for the ordering mens actions in all states and conditions of life, from the highest to the lowest; and enforce each part of our duty from religious motives: Such as are the obedience due to God, our Creator and Governor, the rewards which attend righteousness, and the punishments

ments which follow wickedness by God's just appointment, both in this world and in the next: In which respect this book has much the advantage above all the moral tracts of the philosophers, in that it presses the practice of our duty from the principles of religion, whereas they persuade us to virtue by arguments taken from the agreeableness of it, to our reason and the dignity of our nature, without taking notice of the authority which God has over us, and whose vicegerent our reason and conscience is, and the obedience which his laws challenge from us, which way soever his will and pleasure is notified to us, whether by the inward dictates of our own mind, or the outward voice of his prophets, and messengers [h]. We find *Solomon*

---

[h] Duplex est regula humanorum actuum, Ratio humana, & Deus; sed Deus est prima regula, a qua etiam humana Ratio regulanda est; & ideo virtutes Theologicæ excellentiores sunt virtutibus moralibus. *Aquin* 2da 2dæ qu. 23. *Art.* 6.

lays

the HOLY SCRIPTURES. 141

lays down this rule as the foundation of all his instructions ⁿ, *the fear of the Lord is the beginning of wisdom.* This is a true and solid principle of an universal probity and integrity both of mind and action; it is such as the meanest is capable of apprehending the force of, and being convinced by it. Whereas the notions of philosophers are only fine speculations to amuse men of subtilty and leisure, and not fitted for the use of ordinary capacities: According to *Tully*'s own observation recorded by *Lactantius,* ⁰ *Philosophia est res abhorrens à multitudine. It disdains to condescend to vulgar apprehensions.* But yet the meanest have souls to be saved as well as the greatest, and that institution must needs be defective which doth not answer the necessities of the far greater part of mankind.

ⁿ Prov. i. 7.
⁰ *Institut.* 1. 3. c. 24. v. *Ciceron. initio. l.* 2. *Tusc. Quæst.* Philosophia est paucis contenta judicibus, Multitudinem consulto fugiens, &c.

The

The great sayings of the Philosophers are apt to strike us with admiration at the first hearing, and perhaps prevail with many of our own age to be of *Julian the Apostate's* [*] opinion, who did not stick to prefer the precepts of *Phocylides, Theognis,* and *Isocrates,* before the *Proverbs of Solomon.* But when we thoroughly examine the maxims of these, and such like practical treatises, of the heathen philosophers, we shall find many of them to be rather vainglorious boasts, or the high flights of a fanciful eloquence, than the words of truth and soberness. They are such as the authors of them would never abide by when they came to trial: And what force can we then suppose them to have, toward the reforming of habitual offenders? To tell such persons that they act in contradiction to their reason, and below the dignity of their nature, is to

[*] Apud Cyrillum, contr. Julian. *l.* 7. *p.* 224. Edit. Spanheim.

make them accountable only to themselves; and conscience is but an empty name, unless we suppose that it binds men over to appear before a higher Tribunal. So faint are the persuasives and feeble the reproofs of philosophy, when compared with the instructions and motives contained in the books of *Proverbs*, which being so peculiarly adapted to the meanest capacities, I would particularly recommend it to their frequent reading and diligent perusal.

The design of the book of *Ecclesiastes* is to convince us of the vanity of all things here below, and that from the experience of one who had tried what satisfaction could be found in all manner of worldly enjoyments, and was acquainted with the extravagancies of *madness and folly*[b], as well as with the mysteries of wisdom and knowledge. This great prince, who had tried all things, instructs us not to set our

[b] Eccles. i. 17.

DIRECTIONS *for reading*

hearts too much upon the things of this world, as being empty and unsatisfactory in the enjoyment, and at last ending in *vexation of spirit:* Nor to promise ourselves too much happiness in any worldly blessings, for then we shall be sure to find ourselves disappointed: But to use the good things of this world with sobriety and moderation in respect to ourselves, with submission and thankfulness to God, and with charity to our neighbours [c], always remembring that the *fashion of this world passes away,* and the flower of youth soon decays and withers: And this consideration should engage [d] us to consecrate the best of our years to the service of God, whilst we have a quick and lively sense of his blessings; and not defer the thoughts of religion till *the evil days come,* till old age steal upon us,

---

[c] *See* Ecclef. iii. 11, 12, 13, 14. v. 1, &c. vii. 13, 14. ix 7. xi. 1.
[d] Ecclef. xii. 1, &c.

(which

(which he admirably defcribes) when we are come to the dregs of life, and death is juft ready to feize us, after which comes judgment, and we muft give a ftrict account to God of all our actions.

This is the fubftance and main defign of this book; which if it were ferioufly read, and confidered, would be an effectual prefervative againft the inordinate love of this world, which is the root of all the evil that abounds in it. And to prevent the ill ufe which men of corrupt minds are apt to make of fome paffages in it, I fhall juft obferve, that thofe who will read this book with profit ought to have a regard to the main fcope and drift of it, which is plainly fet down in the conclufion of the whole [e], and not lay hold on one fingle fcrap, or fentence, which they think doth countenance a carelefs and licentious life. The reader that will

[e] Chap. xii. 13, 14.

fix his eye upon the principal defign of this book, will eafily perceive that the contradictory opinions which are mentioned in it, are only a reprefentation of the feveral fentiments of mankind concerning providence and their own fouls, or elfe fhew the various thoughts which *Solomon* himfelf had toffed up and down in his own mind, which at laft came to the refolution wherewith he clofes his book. The fcope and ufefulnefs of which is fo fully made out by our excellent expofitor, the Lord Bifhop of *Ely*, in his *Paraphrafe and Commentary* upon this book, that I fhall rather refer the reader to that ufeful treatife, than enlarge any further upon this fubject.

CHAP.

CHAP. VI.

Concerning the Book of Psalms, *and their Usefulness.*

THE book of *Psalms* deserves to be considered by itself, as being esteemed by pious men in all ages, the great storehouse of devotion, and making up a principal part of the public worship both in the *Jewish* and *Christian* Church. Among the *Jews* they were used at the time of their sacrifices, which were the most solemn part of the *Jewish* worship [d]. The Evangelists inform us that our Saviour and his disciples *sung a Hymn* after the paschal supper [e], which learned men suppose to have been the same collection of *Psalms* which the *Jews* used

[d] *See* 1 Chron. xvi. 40, 41. Ecclus. l. 16, 17, 18.
[e] Math. xxvi. 30.

upon that solemnity. St. *Paul* exhorts the *Colossians* that the *word of God should dwell richly in them*, and particularly recommends the *Psalms* to their frequent use [f]. St. *Jerome* [g] compares the singing of *Psalms* in the publick assemblies of Christians in his time, to the heavenly Hallelujahs, which resembled the *voice of great thunderings*, mentioned *Rev.* xix. 6. and tells [h] us, that the husbandman [i] and common artificers refreshed themselves in the midst of their work, and sweetned their labours with singing the *Psalms* of *David*, and at once served God, and attended upon the duties of their calling; from all which it appears, that the book of *Psalms* was designed by God for the per-

[f] Coloss. iii. 16.
[g] *Præfat. in* l. 2. *Comment. in Epist. ad* Galat.
[h] *Epist.* 17. *ad* Marcellam. *vid. etiam* Theodoret. *Præf. in* Psalm. & Chrysost. *de Pænitent. Hom.* 6.
[i] Γεωργοῦμεν αἰνοῦντες, πλέομεν ὑμνοῦντες. Clem. Alex. Strom. *l.* 5. *p.* 720.

petual

the HOLY SCRIPTURES. 149
petual ufe of the Church, to be both a pattern and treafure of devotion, at once to enlighten our minds and warm our affections, and teach us *to pray* and praife God *with the spirit, and with the underftanding alfo.*

There is an agreeable variety in the compofure of the *Pfalms*, which are all very beautiful and proper in their feafons, and fuited to the feveral circumftances of devout minds. Some of them inftruct us to give God the glory *due unto his name,* and *praife him according to his excellent greatnefs,* as it is made manifeft in the works of creation and providence, as particularly the 8th, the 19th, the 33d, the 103d, the 104th, the 107th, and the 148th. Others fhew forth his marvellous loving-kindnefs to his Church, to Jacob *his people, and* Ifrael *his inheritance;* and foretel the glories of Chrift's coming, and his kingdom. Of which fort are, the 2d, 45th, 68th, 72d,

72d, 78th, 96th, 98th, 105th, 106th 110th, 111th, 136th, and many more. Again, some *Psalms* declare the excellency of God's law, which he hath given us *to be a light to our feet, and a guide to our paths*, and shew the happiness of those who live under the conduct of it. Such are, *Psalm* the 1st, 19th and above all the 119th, which consists of the highest encomiums of God's law, and the most earnest prayers for grace to understand and practise it. At other times the *Psalmist* directs us how to humble ourselves in the sight of God, to implore the pardon of our sins, and help in the time of trouble: Of which kind the most principal *Psalms* are, the 25th, 51st, 130th, 141st, 143d. *Lastly*, In many *Psalms* he exhorts us to submit to God's will in all events, and put our trust in his mercy, *to tarry God's leisure* [z], as he sometimes expresses it, who *will never fail those*

[z] Psal. xxvii. 14.

that

that seek him, and *is the helper of the friendless.* Of which sort the most remarkable *Psalms* are, the 9th, 10th, and 11th. Not to mention many others, in several of which the *Psalmist* instructs us not to regard ourselves only; but likewise to be *mindful of the afflictions of* Joseph, and to pray to God to *deliver* Israel *out of all his troubles.*

So rich a store-house is the book of *Psalms* of all kinds of devotion, and able to furnish every pious soul with holy meditations suitable to his present circumstances, consisting both of the most affectionate prayers and intercessions, and exalted strains of praise and thanksgiving. So deservedly is that divine author stiled *the sweet Psalmist of* Israel [h], as being the greatest author and pattern of spiritual devotion; whose soul was touched with a heavenly flame, *his heart and his flesh rejoiced in the liv-*

[h] 2 Sam. xxiii. 1.

ing God [1]. *With his whole heart he sung songs, and loved him that made him,* as the son of *Syrach* gives his character [k], He *made the praises of God glorious,* and was inspired to sanctify poetry and music, to rescue them from that profane use to which they are commonly debased, and employ them upon the noblest subjects, the glories of God, and the grateful acknowledgments of men for his mercies.

The *Psalms* being so excellently fitted to raise our devotions, it is very fit to obviate all objections, that may be made against the use of them. Two of the principal prejudices against them I shall briefly consider.

The first is the *frequent imprecations which are to be found in the* Psalms, which seem not to favour of the true spirit of devotion, but rather to proceed from passion and

---

[1] Psal. lxxxiv. 2.
[k] Ecclus. xlvii. 8.

revenge; and are thought by some to be contrary to the express commands of Christ[1].

This objection I have considered and answered at large in a former treatise[m], and shall not here repeat what I have there delivered, but shall only suggest to the reader two observations, and leave him to apply them to the several imprecations that are to be met with in the *Psalms*.

1. It is not inconsistent with Christian Charity to wish and pray for the prosperity of the righteous; and in order to that, for the disappointment of the devices of the wicked, especially when they are public enemies and disturbers of the peace of the community. Nor, 2. Is it unlawful to pray, that God's glory may be made manifest by his sending some remarkable judgment upon notorious offenders, in order to their

---

[1] Math. v. 43.
[m] Answer to five Letters, Chap. v.

own amendment, and for a terror to others.

The second objection is made against the use of the *Psalms, as a standing office of publick worship*; against which it is pretended, that since they were composed upon particular exigencies relating to the times and circumstances of their several authors, they cannot be so suitable either to the public state of the present Church, or the private necessities of particular Christians.

In answer to which objection it is to be considered, that we join in the public service of the Church, not as private persons, but as a religious society; and therefore as members of the same mystical body, we ought *to rejoice with those that do rejoice, and mourn with those that mourn:* that is, we ought to return thanks to God, not only for his private favours to ourselves, but likewise for his public mercies conferred upon our brethren: And in like manner we we ought to be mindful of their wants and afflictions, as well as our own, and implore God's help and assistance for all those that are in any trouble or adversity. Granting therefore that some of the deprecatory or thankgiving *Psalms* may not suit the particular circumstances of each private person; yet since there will be always some among the faithful to whose condition they may be fitly applied, we may exercise that Spirit of universal charity in the use of them, which is the peculiar badge of our Christian profession at all times, and the qualification of mind especially required of us, when we join together in the public worship, the most solemn mark or badge of Christian Communion and Fellowship.

To which we may add this further consideration, that according to the general sense and exposition of the universal Church, the prayers against temporal enemies which we meet

meet with in the *Pfalms*, ought to be applied in a myftical fenfe to our conflicts with our fpiritual adverfaries: And the thankfgivings for temporal mercies do in a more fublime fenfe relate to that great deliverance of mankind from fin and death, accomplifhed by our Lord and Saviour. In whom not only all the promifes of the *old Teftament* receive their utmoft completion [d], but likewife all the remarkable occurrences relating to the eminent perfons of thofe times, were fo many types and *figures of him that was to come*, and of the redemption which he was to accomplifh. And this way of expounding feveral paffages in the *Pfalms*, is authorized by Chrift himfelf, who applies thofe words of the *Pfalmift* [e] *they hated me without a caufe,* and [f] *he that eats bread with me hath lift up his*

[d] 2 Cor. i. 20.
[e] Pfal. xxxv. 19.
[f] Pfal. xli. 9.

hee.

heel against me; (which in their primary sense are plainly understood of *David*'s enemies) to his own sufferings from the malice of the *Jews*, and the treachery of *Judas*.

CHAP.

CHAP. VII.

Concerning the Prophetical Writings, and their Usefulness.

I Come now in the fourth place to make some observations concerning the prophets, and give directions for the profitable reading of this last part of the *old Testament* writings.

I have elsewhere [f] spoken at large concerning the great design and usefulness of the prophetical writings, and have shewed that they were intended by God chiefly for these three purposes. 1. To admonish the people of their duty, and quicken them to the practice of it, by setting God's judgments and mercies before their eyes. 2. To keep up a sense of providence in their minds. And 3. To foretel the times of the Messias, and prepare

[f] Answer to 5 Letters, chap. iii.

the HOLY SCRIPTURES. 159
mens minds for the reception of him.

I shall not repeat what I have there discoursed upon these heads, but shall only make some further observations upon these books, in order to confirm their divine authority, and shew the chief uses we ought to make of them, and such as we may draw even from the obscurer parts of those writings, where we cannot perhaps fully comprehend the full intent and drift of the writer.

I. And the first observation which I shall recommend to the consideration of the devout reader of the prophets, is this, *that the historical and prophetical writings of the* old Testament *do mutually support and verify each other; and both of them afford us an undeniable proof of God's universal providence.*

This observation I have briefly touched upon already [s], and now I

[s] Chap. i.

shall

shall illustrate and confirm it by instancing in several particulars. We find, for example, the captivity of the ten tribes clearly foretold by *Hosea* [g], *Amos* [h], and *Isaiah* [i], at a considerable distance of time before that calamity came upon them. The seventy years captivity of the two remaining tribes by *Nebuchadnezzar* is as plainly foretold by *Jeremiah* [k] and their restoration under *Cyrus* by *Isaiah* [l]; the exact accomplishment of which prophecies is taken notice of by the sacred writers, who lived several years after these predictions were made [m].

No less remarkable is the succession of the four great monarchies foretold by *Daniel* [n], and particularly the wonderful successes of *Alexander*, together with the division of his monarchy into four kingdoms [o]; the state of the two principal divisions of

[g] Hof. ix. 3. x. 5. xi. 5. xiii. 16. [h] Amos v. 27. vi. 14. vii. 11. [i] Isa. vii. 8. [k] Jer. xxv. 12. xxix. 10. [l] Isa. xliv. 28. [m] 2 Chr. xxxvi. 22. Ezra. i. 1. [n] Dan. ii. 39, 40. *and* Ch. vii. [o] Dan. viii. 4, 22. *and* Ch. xi. 3, 4.

that

that empire, under the kings of *Syria* and *Egypt* [p], the alliances they should make with each other, and the small success which these alliances should have toward the ending the differences between them: And to name no more particulars, the profanation of the temple under *Antiochus Epiphanes*, one of those kings. All which particulars were so punctually foretold by *Daniel* above three hundred years before several of them came to pass, that *Porphyry* [q], a most bitter enemy to Christianity, had no other way to evade the force of this argument for the truth of the Scriptures, but by asserting that the book of *Daniel* was forged after the times of *Antiochus Epiphanes*. An absurd and groundless conceit! since it is certain, that the whole body of the *old Testament* writings was translated into *Greek* before the time of *Antiochus*; so that it would have been a very easy matter to discover any forgery of this kind. Besides

[p] Dan. xi. 5, &c. [q] *Vid.* Hieron. *Præf. in* Dan.

that, it appears by the testimony of *Josephus* [a], (and the story, as it is there related, has several circumstances which sufficiently attest the truth of it) that the *Jews* shewed this very prophecy to *Alexander the Great*, as he passed through their country, and thereupon obtained several privileges and immunities from him.

These, and several other prophecies, carrying along with them such an undeniable evidence of their truth, and divine original, will afford many useful remarks to the attentive and devout readers.

1. They warrant the accomplishment of those parts of the prophetical writings which remain yet to be fulfilled; forasmuch as both the plain and the obscure prophecies were uttered by the same Spirit, and particularly the *Revelation* in the *new Testament*, takes the *old Testament* prophecies, chiefly those of

[a] *Antiq.* l. 11. c. viii.

Daniel,

Daniel, for its platform and groundwork.

2. Thofe prophecies which immediately concern the *Jewifh* ftate, prove that there was a particular providence always attending that nation; and they are an evident accomplifhment of thofe judgments which were denounced againft that people in the law of *Mofes,* whenever they fhould depart from the worfhip and fervice of the true God.

3. They are a fenfible proof of God's univerfal providence, and an evident demonftration that the eternal mind comprehends the whole feries of caufes and effects at one fingle view, fees through all the intricate turnings and windings of human counfels, and over-rules and conducts them to what end he pleafes. *I am God, and there is none like me,* faith he, in the prophet, ° *declaring the end from the beginning, and from ancient times the*

° Ifa. xlvi. 10.

things

things that are not yet done, saying, my counsel shall stand, and I will do all my pleasure. The signal accomplishment of several prophecies uttered many ages beforehand, opens our minds and lets us into that noble contemplation, how God carries on one steady and uniform design without being interrupted by those many changes and chances which are in the world, and that confusion and disorder which appears among several second causes. It convinces us his infinite wisdom does unerringly foresee the most distant and casual events, and makes them all subservient to the carrying on the great ends of providence. That God by his almighty power is able to bring good out of evil, as he did light out of darkness at the beginning of the creation, and to make the rage and fury, the malice and *fierceness of men to turn to his praise*, and his enemies themselves become instrumental in promoting his glory: According-ing to the observation of the wise man, [p] *Thy wisdom, O Lord, reaches from one end to another mightily, and sweetly doth she order all things.*

4. It follows from hence in the fourth place, that the most obscure parts of the prophetical writings ought not to be despised, as if they were altogether useless. For though we should suppose them of no use to the Church at present, yet they may be useful to after-times; and *what they* mean, *though we know not now, yet we may know hereafter.* But besides this, even from the obscurest prophecies we may learn this important truth, that the designs of providence reach from one age to another, and some greater lines of it run through many ages; in all which time there is one design pursued with infinite turnings and great variety of wisdom, all the particular occurrences being directed by a steady and unerring counsel to some

[p] Wisd. viii. 1.

glori-

glorious conclusion, and that with a particular regard to the good of the Church, the point wherein all the great lines of providence do meet as in their center.

And perhaps this is the best use that persons of ordinary capacities can make of the darker prophecies; and it is not only a rash undertaking for any to venture the fathoming those deep things of God, without the necessary helps of learning, and *being able to compare spiritual things with spiritual;* but it is likewise apt to lead such persons into great and dangerous mistakes. So that it highly concerns every one *to think soberly of himself, according to that measure of faith* [q] and knowledge which God hath given him, and *not to be curious in unnecessary matters, nor search out things that are above their strength* [r].

But there are several practical truths of great use for the governing mens lives, which may be learnt from the

[q] Rom. xii. 3.   [r] Ecclus. iii. 21, 23.

obscurer books of the prophets, without undertaking to unfold the particular events therein foretold, or to decypher the persons there described. For example, the *Revelation* may upon many accounts be reckoned one of the obscurest books of all the prophetical writings; but yet without venturing upon a particular explication of the several visions of it, an ordinary reader may receive great edification from those noble hymns offered up there to God and Christ [a], and may likewise discover very useful truths frequently recommended in it; such as the adoration of the one supreme God in opposition to all creature-worship [b]; the relying upon the merits of Christ only for pardon, sanctification and salvation [c]; that we ought to wait patiently for Christ's *appearing and his kingdom*, and in an earnest expectation of it, to continue stedfast in

[a] Rev. iv. 8, 11. v. 9, 10, 12, 13. vii. 12. xv. 3, 4.
[b] Rev. ix. 20. xiv. 7. xxi. 8. xxii. 15.
[c] Rev. v. 9. vii. 14. xii. 11. xiii. 18.

the profession of the true faith, and practice of sincere holiness, notwithstanding all the sufferings that may attend a good conscience [d]. And though every ordinary reader should not rashly undertake to determine who *Antichrist* is, that is there described; yet every one may certainly be informed from several passages of that book, of those marks and characters of him, which it most nearly concerns us to take notice of, namely, pride and ambition, and an affectation of worldly pomp and grandeur [e], a cruel and persecuting temper [f], and such as seeks to reduce others rather by force and compulsion, than by reason and argument; the love of ease and softness, and a careless and luxurious life [g] : and that whoever are guilty of these things, they are so far departed from the true Spirit of Christianity. And surely he that takes

[d] Rev. ii. 3, 10, 26. xiii. 10. xiv. 12, 13, xvi. 15.
[e] Rev. xiii. 7. xvii. 4.
[f] Rev. ix. 21. xi. 7. xiii. 7, 10, 15, 17. xvi. 6. xvii. 6. xviii. 20, 24. xix. 2.
[g] Rev. iii. 3. xviii. 3, 7, 9, 12, &c.

the HOLY SCRIPTURES.

warning from the plain and frequent admonitions of this book to avoid these sins, has not wholly lost his labour in reading it, and withal has intitled himself to the *blessing* which is pronounced upon those *who keep the sayings of it* [a].

These uses persons of ordinary capacities may make even of the obscurest parts of the prophetical writings; but I am persuaded that God intended men of better talents should reap greater benefit from a sober and devout search into them: And that as a reward of their thirst after divine truth, he often admits such persons *within the veil*, and gives them the *key of knowledge* wherewith to unlock those sacred treasures of God's hidden counsels. However that be, this one thing is a sufficient reward of their labour, that they have the satisfaction of observing the exact harmony and correspondence that is to be found between the several *symbols*

[a] Rev. i. 3. xxii. 7.

and

and *figurative expreſſions,* which are made uſe of in divers parts of thoſe myſterious writings: Which amounts to a demonſtration, that the prophets were not under illuſions of an enthuſiaſtic heat or roving imagination, but had always ſome certain views which guided and influenced their pen. Accordingly they often word their prophecies with a critical niceneſs of expreſſion, (a remarkable inſtance of which may be ſeen, *Rev.* xii. 3. compared with *Chap.* xiii. 1.) and the *emblems* and figures which they make uſe of are as capable of being reduced under rules, as the terms of any art or ſcience whatſoever.

II. Another particular very obſervable in thoſe prophecies, which relate to the times of the Meſſias, is the *myſtical ſenſe of ſeveral paſſages in them contained under the literal;* of which we may aſſign ſeveral examples. As, 1. when the prophets deſcribe the Meſſias under ſuch characters as have a more immediate aſpect

upon

the HOLY SCRIPTURES. 171

upon some eminent person in or near their own times [e]. 2. When they represent the redemption of mankind, which he was to accomplish, by such expressions as do, in their first and primary sense, allude to some temporal deliverance which God had [f], or would vouchsafe to their own nation [g]. Or, *lastly*, when they set forth the benefits of the Gospel by phrases taken from the forms of divine worship prescribed by their law [h].

Any one that carefully reads the prophets, will quickly be convinced, that the views which they had of future events, reached a great way beyond their own times; and were not confined to the narrow limits of their own nation. I shall prove this

[e] *See* 2 Sam. vii. 14. Psal. ii. 6, 7. Psal. xlv. & lxxii. lxxxix. 26, 27. Hagg. ii. 23. Zech. vi. 11, 12.
[f] *See* Psal. lxviii. 22, 23.
[g] *See* Isa. xl. 3, &c. xlix. 8, &c. lii. 7, &c. liv. 1, &c. lx. 1, &c.
[h] *See* Isa. ii. 1. lxvi. 20, 23. Zech. xiv. 16. 20.

H 2 by

by two plain inftances, out of many that might be alledged.

We will allow that the wonderful reftoration of the *Jewiſh* captivity, and their return into their own land, might be the ground-work, of all thoſe predictions concerning the flouriſhing ſtate of the Church, which we find foretold by *Iſaiah* with a very pompous eloquence, from the 40th chapter to the end of his prophecy. But none can ſay, that all theſe glorious promiſes could in any tolerable ſenſe be accompliſhed in thoſe poor remains of God's choſen people, or thoſe inconſiderable ſucceſſes which they afterwards obtained under the *Maccabees* againſt their enemies: when their condition at beſt, was nothing near ſo proſperous as it had formerly been in the days of *David* and *Solomon*. So that we cannot maintain the truth of ſo conſiderable a part of the *Old Teſtament*, prophecy, but by aſſerting, that the prophet was carried on from his firſt ſubject to a more

the HOLY SCRIPTURES.

more agreeable prospect of the enlargement of the Church under the Gospel, and perhaps foresaw a more flourishing state of it than the world hath yet been blessed with.

A second proof of this point shall be taken from those prophecies of *Isaiah* and *Jeremiah*, which foretel the destruction of *Babylon* [f]; and they both describe it as a decisive stroke which should thoroughly vindicate the cause of oppressed truth and innocence [g], and should put a final period to idolatry [h], and to the miseries and afflictions of God's people [i].

None can with any shew of probability pretend, that any of these ends were attained by the overthrow of the *Babylonian* monarchy by *Cy-*

---

[f] *See* Isa. xiii. 19, 20. Jer. l. 39, 40. li. 64.
[g] *See* Isa. xiv. 1, 2, &c. Jer. l. 34. li. 11, 35, 36.
[h] *See* Isa. xxi 8. xlv. 16. Jer. l. 2, 38. li. 17, 18, 44, 47.
[i] *See* Jer. l. 4, 5, 19, 20.

rus. For neither was *Babylon* itself destroyed till a considerable time after; nor did that great turn of affairs give any remarkable check to idolatry. For the *Persians* were as great strangers to the true God, as the *Babylonians*; this was the only difference between them, that the *Persians* did not worship images [d], but contented themselves with representing the Divine Majesty by the external symbol of fire, or it may be worshipped him in some other of the elements. From whence we may conclude that these prophets had some further event in their view, and took occasion from that remarkable judgment of God upon the *Babylonish* monarchy, the great enemy and oppressor of God's people, to give some

---

[d] Πέςσαι ἀγάλματα καὶ βωμὲς ἐκ ἰδ, ύσίlαι. Strab. 1. 15. *De* Persis *& Medis eadem habet*. Clem. Alex. Protrept. p. 43. A. Ἀγάλματα μὲν Θεῶν ἢ ξύλα καὶ λίθες ὑπειληφασιν, ὥσπερ Ἕλληνες——ἀλλὰ πῦρ τι καὶ ὕδωρ ὡς φιλόσοφοι. Μεῖα πολλὰς μέντοι ὕστερον περιόδες ἰδῶν αἰθρωποειδῆ ἀγάλματα σέβειν αὐτὲς Βηρωσσὸς ἐν τρίτῃ Χαλδαικῶν παρίστησι.

general

general hints of the great downfal of *Antichrift*, the laſt and finiſhing ſtroke of the divine vengeance which ſhall be inflicted upon the adverſaries of God's Church and truth, as it is more fully deſcribed by St. *John* in his *Revelation*.

That a great part of the prophetical writings have a myſtical ſenſe involved under a literal one, is a point generally agreed both by the *Jews* and Chriſtians. When Chriſt and his Apoſtles explained the prophecies of the *Old Teſtament* in this manner, we do not find that the *Jews* contradicted the notion in general, or charged them with miſapplying the particular texts which they alledged, as if they did not relate to the times of the Meſſias. So both parties agreed in this [k], that all the remarkable occurrences of former times were figures of that which ſhould come to paſs in the *latter days*. Accordingly

[k] *See* Dr. *Allix*, againſt the Unitar. c. 2. & 3.

we

we find that the Apoſtles not only argued againſt the *Jews*, from the plain predictions of the prophets, but likewiſe from the rites and ordinances of the *Jewiſh* worſhip [l], as types and figures of the times of the Meſ-ſias, and do further take it for granted, that all the eminent perſons of foregoing ages, and the remarkable paſſages of their lives, did bear ſome reſemblance or repreſentation [m] of *him that was to come.* They ſuppoſe that the preferring *Iſaac* before *Iſhmael*, and *Jacob* before *Eſau*, did prefigure the rejection of the *Jews*, and the calling of the *Gentiles* [n] : they draw a parallel between the ſtate of the *Iſraelites* in the wildernefs, and the condition of Chriſtians during their pilgrimage in this world [o]. And to paſs by many other inſtances, we may obſerve that ſeveral expreſ-

---

[l] *See* Heb. viii. 5. ix. 8, 18.
[m] *See* Heb. ii. 12, 13.
[n] Rom. ix. 6, &c.
[o] Heb. iii, & iv. 1. Cor. x. 1, &c.

sions in the *Revelation* allude to the *Egyptian* bondage [h]; to the apostacy of the ten tribes begun by *Jeroboam*, and increased by the wicked kings who succeeded him [i], to the *Babylonish* captivity, and to the taking away of many *Jews* in the time of *Antiochus Epiphanes* [k]. As so many *præludia*, or forerunners of the days of *Antichrist*, (who is likewise described under the characters of the idolatrous governments, and persecuting princes mentioned in the *Old Testament*) [l], and of the grand apostacy which St. *Paul* foretold [m] should break out, and which that prophecy doth more particularly describe.

These *providential congruities* between the times of the *Old* and *New Testament*, as a learned writer stiles them, do very much confirm the au-

[h] Revel. xi. 6, 8. xii. 6. xv. 3. xvi. 2, 3, 4.
[i] Ibid. ch. ii. 20. xi. 3. 5, 6. Chap. xiv. 8. xviii. 2, 4, &c.
[k] Chap. xi. 2. xiii. 5.
[l] *See* Chap. xiii. &. xviii.
[m] 2 Thess. ii. 3.

thority of both Teſtaments. From hence we learn that the Scriptures comprehend one intire ſcene of providence which reaches from one end of the world to the other: and that God, who is the beginning and end of all things, by various ſteps and degrees purſues one great deſign, namely, The ſetting up the kingdom of his Son, through the ſeveral ages of the world, and will ſtill carry it on by ſuch meaſures as ſeem beſt to his infinite wiſdom, till the great day of the conſummation of all things. Such a gradual opening this wonderful ſcene of providence, is a new argument of that infinite wiſdom which contrived it, and ſo fully juſtifies this myſtical way of propounding it.

Several other conſiderations may be offered that juſtify the wiſdom of God's conduct in fore-ſhewing the times of the new covenant under the types and figures of the old.

1. It was neceſſary that the prophecies relating to the Goſpel, and the ſpi-

spiritual benefits thereof, should be delivered to the *Jews* under the emblems of temporal blessings, and such representations as would appear most glorious in their apprehensions [k] in order to recommend them more powerfully to their carnal minds, and worldly affections. Whereas if the nature of Christ's kingdom had been set forth plainly by the prophets, as it was in itself, they would have received the promises but coldly, and had but a faint desire to see them accomplished. It was the earthly kingdom of the Messias which they set their hearts upon; this raised in their minds an earnest expectation of the *Redeemer of Israel*, and made them such zealous preservers of those holy records, which gave them a title to that glorious promise: whereas if the spiritual nature of Christ's kingdom had been clearly fore-shewed, if the prophets had plainly discovered that

[k] *Loquitur Propheta Figuris, quæ suæ conveniunt ætati*: Calvin. in Isa. lvi. 7.

the

the *Gentiles* were to be *fellow-heirs* with the *Jews,* and *partakers of the same promises,* they would in all probability have slighted and rejected the prophecies concerning the Messias, as they did Christ himself when he appeared.

2. It was requisite that the times of the Gospel should be foretold with some degree of obscurity, and couched under veils and figures, because the *Jews* themselves were to be instruments in bringing about the work of man's redemption by the death and sufferings of the Messias: which if it had been clearly foretold, the prophecies would have defeated their own accomplishment, and we cannot suppose, humanly speaking, that the *Jews* when they were thus forewarned would have had a hand in *crucifying their king,* and despitefully using him that was the hope, the expectation, and the *glory of Israel:* whereas *because they knew him not, nor yet the voices*

voices of the prophets, they fulfilled them in condemning him, as St. Paul tells them [1].

3. The veil drawn over the prophecies, is very serviceable to that wonderful conduct of providence, in appointing the *Jews* to be witnesses and conservators of those very prophecies which shew the unreasonableness of their unbelief. They carry the Christians books and evidences for them, as St. *Austin* [m] acutely observed, and God hath therefore dispersed them over the world, that they might bear witness to that truth which they themselves refuse to acknowledge, whilst they continue zealous assertors of those divine oracles, which prove that our Jesus, whom they deny, is the very Christ. *O God, how wonderful art thou in thy works! through the greatness of thy power shall thy enemies become liars unto*

[1]. Acts xiii. 27.
[m] *In* Psalm lviii. (lix. secund. Hebr.) & *alibi*.

thee [n],

thee[a], and stand condemned out of their own mouths.

III. A third particular which I would defire the pious reader to obferve, in the writings of the prophets, (and which is that part of them that is beft fuited to common capacities) is that *holy zeal wherewith they reprove the vices of the times they lived in,* and thofe pathetic exhortations, whereby they perfuade finners to amend their ways, and break off their fins by a fincere repentance. Here they give us a true pattern of that courage and conftancy, that zeal and fervency, wherewith we ought to maintain the caufe of religion, when they rebuke the vices of the great ones, as well as of the meaneft, without fear or flattery; when they reprove great and hainous offences, with an awful authority, with great feverity againft fin, and yet great compaffion towards finners: and exhort them to repent, and

[a] Pfalm lxvi. 3.

turn

turn to God, by all the powerful perfuafives of an holy eloquence. Firſt *befeeching them by the mercies of God*, by all that he has done for them, by the obligations he has laid upon them, and the right that he has to their fervice: recounting his paſt favours towards them, and renewing his gracious promifes for the time to come: and if thefe gentle methods will not prevail with finners, they then reprefent to them the greatnefs of God's majeſty, the dread of his power, the fiercenefs of his anger, their own monſtrous ingratitude and incorrigiblenefs, in abufing his mercies, defpifing his judgments, refifting his Spirit, and rendering ineffectual all thofe methods which divine wifdom itfelf could make ufe of, to recover finners from the error of their ways. Thefe difcourfes verify that faying of the prophet *Jeremiah* [o], that *God's Word* in the mouth of his prophets *is as a fire*,

[o] Jer. xxiii. 29.

which

which makes its way through all opposition, *and like a hammer that breaks the rocks in pieces;* is able to subdue the most obdurate heart, if it be seriously attended to, and to beat down the confidence of the most daring offender.

We may farther observe, that these moral discourses of the prophets favour very much of a true and evangelical spirit of piety and holiness. They exhort men not to lay too much stress upon the practical observance of the ceremonial law ᵐ; but to *fulfil the righteousness* chiefly intended by it, *in walking not after the flesh, but after the Spirit.* The *Jews* think that the chief strength of their cause lies in this point, that God himself has declared that the law of *Moses* should be of perpetual obligation. But these discourses of the prophets afford an unanswerable confutation to this their pretence.

ᵐ Isa. i. 11. xvi. 3. Jerem. vii. 21, 22, 23. Hos. vi. 6. Amos v. 21. Mic. vi. 6, 7, 8.

For there we fee the prophets themfelves, who lived under the law, fhewing men a more excellent way of pleafing God, than by the formal acts of an external obedience, and plainly foretelling ᵇ that the *Mofaical* covenant fhould at laft give way to a better, which I come in the next place to confider.

ᵇ Jer. xxxi. 31.

C H A P.

CHAP. VIII.

Observations upon the Gospels, in order to the more useful reading that part of Holy Scripture.

I Proceed to discourse of the particular uses we are to make of the writings of the *New Testament,* as it is commonly called, because the benefits therein contained are conveyed to us by the death of Christ, who has as it were bequeathed them to us in this his last will and testament. But the title of those books might more properly be translated *the new covenant* [c], as it is distinguished from the former *covenant,* which God made with the *Jews,* by the ministry and mediation of *Moses.* That was a law, taking the word in its proper sense, requiring strict obe-

[c] Διαθήκη.

dience under severe penalties: Or a *covenant of works*, denouncing an irreversible curse upon those who did not continue in an exact obedience to all the duties therein commanded [d]. Whereas the *new covenant* is a *covenant of grace*, and thereupon is called *the gift of grace and abundance of grace* [e], because it makes merciful allowances for the unavoidable frailties of human nature, and sets forth Christ to be a propitiation for the sins of all those who truly repent, and endeavour to please by a sincere, though imperfect obedience. *The law was given by Moses, but grace and truth came by Jesus Christ* [f]: The Gospel is there called *grace* in opposition to the severity of the law, which denounced judgment against great offences without mercy; and *truth*, whereby it is distinguished from the figures of the law, which was but a *shadow of good things to come* [g].

[d] Deut. xxvii. 26.
[e] Rom. v. 15, 17.
[f] John i. 17.
[g] Heb. x. 1.

I have

I have already observed [h], that the books of the *Old Testament* give two different schemes or representations of the *Jewish* religion; and according to those different views of it, St. *Paul* gives very different characters of that institution. Sometimes he calls the law spiritual [i], at other times he stiles it [k] a *carnal commandment*. The ambiguity of the word Νόμος, as it is taken for the *Jewish* law under its several acceptations, is, I conceive, a principal cause of the obscurity of St. *Paul*'s discourses upon the subject of justification, and of the many different opinions, which have been advanced concerning that point. It seems most probable that the word Law, as it is opposed in the *New Testament* to the Gospel, usually signifies that system of laws and ordinances, which were the terms of the *covenant* made

[h] Supr. chap. iv.
[k] Hebr. vii. 16.
[i] Rom. vii. 14.

with

the HOLY SCRIPTURES. 189
with the *Jews* at mount *Sinai* [1] : Especially as their extent and obligation was understood and explained in the time of Christ and the Apostles, both by the dictates of the *Jewish Rabbies*, and the concurring practice of the people [m]. These were a body of laws chiefly intended for the government of that common-wealth; which according to the nature of all political laws, laid a greater stress upon the outward act of obedience, than the inward sincerity of the mind: It was rather designed as a restraint to the *lawless and disobedient*, than as a rule of perfection to *the righteous* [n] : It did not expressly promise any internal assistances [o], nor future rewards [p], nor did it offer any method of propitiation for great and presumptuous offences. In which respects the Apostle saith, that

---

[1] *See* Act xv. 5. Galat. iii. 17. Rom. iii. 19.
[m] *See* Rom. ix. 32. x. 3. Matth. v. 20. & ch. xv. 11, 12. [n] 1 Tim. i. 9. Gal. iii. 19. [o] *See* Rom. iv. 4. & ch. xi. 6. [p] *V.* Heb. vii. 19. viii. 6.

the

the *law was weak through the flesh* [q], that it *was the strength of sin* [r], that it *could not justify* [s] *nor give life* [t], that the *Jews were in the flesh* [u], in a carnal state, and *trusted in the flesh* [w], in fleshly privileges [d], and *carnal ordinances* [e]: That the law was a *dead letter* [f], whereas the Gospel was *spirit and life* [g]: That it *worketh wrath* [h], that it involves those that rely upon it *under a curse* [i], that it was *weak and unprofitable* [k], *made nothing perfect*, nor could attain the end which the zealous contenders for it proposed to themselves, that is, It could neither justify them here, nor save them hereafter. Taking the *law* in the forementioned sense, we may give a satisfactory account why the Apostle speaks of it in such undervaluing

[q] Rom. viii. 3. [r] 1 Cor. xv. 56. [s] Rom. iii. 20. Gal. ii. 16. [t] Gal. iii. 21. [u] Rom. vii. 5. [w] Phil. iii. 3. [d] Ibid. v. 5, 6. [e] Heb. ix. 10. [f] Rom. vii. 5, 6. [g] Rom. viii. 2. 2 Cor. iii. 6. [h] Rom. iv. 15. [i] Gal. iii. 10. [k] Heb. vii. 18, 19.

terms;

terms; and may eafily affign the reafon why he excludes *works* from having any relation to our juftification. And the famous prophecy of *Jeremy*, where ᵐ he ftates the difference between the *old* and *new covenant*, does very much confirm this interpretation. There he exprefsly calls the *former covenant*, that which God *made with our fathers when he brought them out of the land of Egypt*; and then reckons up the advantages which the *new covenant* fhould have above it; wherein God promifes that he *would put his laws into their inward parts, and write them in their hearts*; that is, He would require inward purity inftead of external obedience, and a reafonable fervice in the place of carnal ordinances, and would put his fpirit within them to enable them to perform their duty heartily and fincerely. It follows, *I will be their God, and they fhall be my people, and their fins and iniquities*

ᵐ Jer. xxxi. 31.

will

will I remember no more; that is, God would set forth Christ to be a perfect propitiation for sins to all those that truly repent and turn from their evil ways, and thereby assure them of his favour and loving kindness, and that nothing shall separate them from an interest in his love. This is that second and better *covenant,* as St. *Paul* calls it [a], of which Christ is the Mediator: *Established upon better Promises,* namely, [b] the clearer revelation of a future state, and more plentiful effusion of the divine grace [b], than was granted under the law: And consisting of more excellent precepts, and those recommended to our practice by the most engaging motives, such as are taken from this consideration, that the Son of God *came down from heaven, that he might give life unto the world* [c].

[a] Heb. viii. 6, 7. [b] 2 Tim. i. 10. [b] See Isa. xliv. 3. liv. 13. Ezek. xi. 19. xxxvi. 27. Joel ii. 28. Joh. vii. 39. Gal. iii. 2. Ephes. i. 13.
[c] Joh. vi. 33.

These

These *glad tidings of peace and salvation* which the Gospel brings unto us, for our comfort and instruction, are delivered to us in the writings of the Apostles and holy pen-men of the *New Testament*, to whose words we ought to *give the most earnest heed* and attention; for *how shall we escape, if we neglect so great salvation, which at the first began to be spoken by the Lord, and was confirmed to us by them that heard him*°?

The usefulness of which writings I come now to consider, and shall divide them into two sorts. 1. The Gospels which contain the history of our Lord's life and doctrine; and 2. The Acts and Epistles, which give us an account of the preaching of the Apostles, and the manner how they propagated Christianity in the world.

In discoursing upon the first head, I shall in the first place consider the

° Heb. ii. 3.

prin-

principal matters contained in the Gospels, and then the manner how they are delivered.

The principal matters contained in the Gospels may be reduced to these four heads. 1. Our Lord's doctrine. 2. His miracles. 3. His manner of life, and 4. The circumstances of his death.

1. Our Lord's doctrine. He came down from heaven to shew us the way thither, to *bring us from darkness to light, and from the power of Satan to God:* To instruct us in the knowledge of the true God, and the means whereby we might approve ourselves to him. And this he did two ways; more plainly and openly in his sermons and other discourses; more obscurely and reservedly in his parables.

Of all his discourses, that which I shall chiefly take notice of is, that glorious, full, and admirable sermon which he delivered upon the mount, and is contained in the 5th, 6th, and

and 7th chapters of St. *Matthew*. This divine difcourfe comprehends in it the very marrow and quinteffence of Chriftianity, and ought to be the daily fubject of every good Chriftian's reading and meditation, till he has copied it into his life and converfation.

The great defign of our Saviour in this fermon, is to exhort us to *cleanfe ourfelves from all filthinefs both of flefh and fpirit*; to bring forth the fruits of righteoufnefs out of a pure confcience: To purify our hearts from all corrupt affections, as thofe that would approve themfelves to that God whofe property it is to fearch the heart, and who knows the moft fecret thoughts and defires that lie lurking in the retired corners of it.

And that men might not fatisfy themfelves with faying that their heart is right toward God, he further teaches us, that we muft teftify the fincerity of our inward difpofitions by bringing forth the vifible fruits

fruits of good works, just as the life and goodness of the tree is known by its fruit: That we must demonstrate the reality of our inward love toward God, by real acts of mercy and charity to our brethren: That we must shew all kindness to all men, and do injury to none; that we must not *render evil for evil,* but *love our enemies, and do good to them that hate us,* in imitation of our heavenly Father, who is the most glorious instance of free bounty, of unwearied patience, and of unconfined mercy.

In short the great aim of this, and all our Saviour's discourses is, to give men a true notion of *pure and undefiled religion*; and to preserve it from those two cankers which are apt to eat out the very life and heart of it, which are *hypocrisy* and *spiritual pride.* Those were the reigning sins of the *Scribes* and *Pharisees,* whereby they had corrupted the very vitals of the *Jewish* religion, and which

which rendered all their high pretences to godlineſs of none effect, and unſerviceable to any of the true ends of religion.

To prevent mens being guilty of hypocriſy, our Saviour often puts them in mind that *God is a Spirit, and they that ſerve him, muſt worſhip him in ſpirit and in truth* [p] *:* That the true way to make the *outſide of the cup clean, is to waſh the inſide firſt* [q] *:* That we muſt not content ourſelves with appearing righteous [r] in the eyes of the world, nor greedily *ſeek the praiſe of men, but that which comes from God* [s], the moſt righteous and uncorrupt judge, by whoſe ſentence we muſt ſtand or fall, and who alone is *able to ſave and to deſtroy*.

Nor was he leſs induſtrious to check the beginnings of ſpiritual pride, a ſubtile and dangerous enemy, which very often lurks under

[p] Joh. iv. 24.   [q] Mat. xxiii. 26.   [r] Ibid. ver. 28.   [s] John v. 44.

the difguife of mortification and renouncing of the world. Pride indeed was always detefted as an unreafonable and unfeemly vice, but yet the world was never taught the true leffon of humility, until our Saviour came to inftruct it. The foundation of Chriftianity is laid in that divine truth * *that Jefus Chrift came into the world to fave finners; a faithful faying and worthy of all acceptation,* as the Apoftle truly ftiles it ᶠ: A faying more valuable than whole volumes of philofophy and human wifdom, which both difcovers our diftemper, and directs us where to find a cure. How different from this felf-denying maxim were the notions of the philofophers? among whom no principle was more current than this, *that virtue and happinefs were in mens own power* ᵍ. They that were of this opinion

---

ᵉ *See* John iii. 16. Matth. xviii. 11.
ᶠ 1 Tim. i. 15.
ᵍ It is true that the Philofophers did fometimes, when they fpoke more correctly, acknowledge *divine*

the HOLY SCRIPTURES. 199

opinion could have but little fenfe of the inbred corruption of human nature, and they who were not fenfible that they were fick, would not be very forward to feek out for a phyfician. Their wife man had *no need of repentance* ʳ, and confequently was not under any apprehenfion of *the wrath to come.* As he did not place his happinefs in God, fo neither did he lift up his foul to him. He was willing to believe that *virtue was its own reward,* and made ufe of this fpecious fhew of prefent fatisfaction, only to hide his diftruft of a future reward ˢ.

I 4   Thefe

vine affiftances, as hath been fhewed by learned men, particularly by Mr. *Dodwell, Prolegom. ad lib. D. Stearn. de obftinatione Sect.* 55, 56   But the general ftrain of their writings takes no notice of any fuch thing, and the common readers underftood the expreffions they ufe concerning felf-fufficiency, in a fenfe exclufive of it, as appears by that noted expreffion of *Horace,* Lib 1. Ep. xviii.

Hoc fatis eft orare Jovem ——
Det vitam, det opes, æquum animum ipfe parabo.

ʳ *Sapiens nihil facit quod non debet, nihil prætermittit quod debet.* Senec. de Clement. *l.* 2 *c* 7.

ˢ *Socrates* himfelf fpeaks very doubtfully of this matter, in his *apology,* whofe words are thus tranflated

These were some of the great attainments of the Heathen philosophers, or rather *great swelling words of vanity*, which their pride suggested to them, utterly void of truth and soberness. Whereas the great design of all our Saviour's instructions was to exalt God, and to humble man. To this end he taught men [i] that they were naturally slaves to sin and error, that he was *come a light unto the world, that whosoever believes in him should not abide in* darkness [k]: That by his dying for them [l] he was to redeem them

---

stated by *Cicero*, *Tusc. Quæst.* l. i.. *Tempus est jam hinc abire me, ut moriar, vos ut vitam agatis: utrum autem sit melius Dii immortales sciunt: hominem quidem scire arbitror neminem,* Nor does *Tully* in that place, or in his book *de Senectute* speak with greater assurance. *Seneca* labours under the same uncertainty, as will appear to any that compare the places where he asserts the soul's immortality, with his 54th *Epistle* and 19th Ch. *de Consolat. ad Marciam.* Even *Antoninus* himself could come to no resolution in this point. *See l.* 4. *n.* 15. Edit. Oxon.

[i] John iii. 6.   [k] John xii. 46.   [l] Matth. xx. 28.   John vi. 51.

from

from the power of sin, and the *wages of it, death* eternal; and by his living in them [m] he was to enable them to *bring forth fruit unto holiness, the end* of which would be *everlasting life*. He instructs us not to be proud of our spiritual attainments, that when we have done our best, still we ought to say, *we are unprofitable servants* [n] : Forasmuch as all *our righteousness is but as filthy rags*, and our best actions have so great an alloy of sin and imperfection, that they cannot be acceptable to so holy and pure a being as God almighty is, but only thro' the all-sufficient merits of his Son, *in whom* alone *he is well pleased*.

To conclude this point, the sum of our Saviour's preaching consists in inculcating this one great and fundamental truth of Christianity, that *we are nothing, and God is all in all*; it is his word that enlightens our

---

[m] John xiv. 19. xv. 4, 5.   [n] Luke xvii. 10.

minds, his Spirit directs our wills, his providence orders our affairs, his grace guides us here, and his mercy muſt bring us to heaven hereafter. So that if we will needs glory, we muſt *glory only in the Lord,* we muſt acknowledge that all good things come from him, and nothing is truly valuable but what renders us accepted with him.

Theſe diſcourſes ſhew that the author of them *knew what was in man,* was perfectly acquainted with all the weakneſſes and infirmities of his conſtitution, and underſtood how to apply ſuitable remedies to his moſt prevailing diſtempers.

Thus I have endeavoured briefly to repreſent the great aim and tendency of our Saviour's doctrine, and ſhewed how much it exceeds the higheſt attainments of human wiſdom, becauſe it teaches us to know God and ourſelves, to *give him the honour which is due unto his name,* and to hum-

humble ourselves before him, as sinful dust and ashes.

I proceed to take a short view of our Saviour's *parables*, and shew the great usefulness of them.

It was the custom of the wise men among the ancients to cloath their instructions in apt stories and suitable comparisons: Such is the parable of *Jotham* °, and that very appofite one of *Nathan* to *David* ᵖ; this they did at once to please and to instruct, to excite mens attention by gratifying their curiosity, and to quicken their memory by entertaining their fancy. Our Saviour took this method to recommend his weighty instructions, and make them sink deeper into the minds of his auditors. The same method was likewise very proper for another purpose, namely, to deliver the mysteries of the Gospel with some degree of obscurity and reserve; which he did

° Judg. iv. 8.   ᵖ 2 Sam. xii. 1.

I 6   both

both to excite mens induſtry in ſearching further into the deep things of God, and withal to puniſh the ſloth and negligence of thoſe who grudge taking any pains to learn God's will and their own duty. This reaſon you may find our Saviour himſelf aſſigns why he ſpake to the multitude in parables, *Matth.* xiii. 10, &c. Theſe were the reaſons why our Saviour choſe to convey his inſtructions in parables. And we may obſerve in general concerning them, firſt that they have a pleaſing variety ſuited to mens different apprehenſions and capacities, and in the next place that there is an extraordinary decency, and if I may ſo expreſs it, a *genteelneſs*, which runs through them all. Our Saviour puts the caſe in all his parables on the charitable ſide, and makes the moſt favourable repreſentation of things which the matter will bear. In the parable of the *ten virgins* [e], he

[e] Mat. xxv. 2.

ſup-

the HOLY SCRIPTURES.

suppoſes the number of the wiſe to be equal to that of the fooliſh. In the parable of the *loſt ſheep* [f], he ſuppoſes but one of an hundred to go aſtray: And yet the *good ſhepherd* is content to leave all the reſt, and go in queſt after that ſingle ſtraggler. In the third place there is an exact *decorum* obſerved in all Chriſt's parables, and every thing that is ſpoken is fitted to the character of the perſon who ſpeaks it: A beauty which the critics [r] look upon as the greateſt ornament of a poem, and which of its ſelf is ſufficient to make it heard, or read with delight and admiration: And therefore, I hope, it may recommend our Saviour's parables to the nice and delicate taſte of our modern wits, who are apt to think every thing in Scripture ſo mean and flat, as not to be worth their reading.

[f] Luke xv. 4. [r] Si Plauſoris eges—Ætatis cujuſque notandi ſunt tibi mores. *Horat. Art. Poet.* v. 154. *etiam* v. 319.

Thus

Thus much we observe in general concerning our Saviour's parables: Let us now take a brief view of some of the more remarkable ones.

To begin with the parable of the [b] *prodigal:* In what lively colours [i] doth our Saviour there describe the follies and madness of an extravagant course of life, and the hardships and miseries it usually betrays men to; how repentance is a man's *coming to himself* [k] again, and first of all returning to his own right senses, and then to God and his duty. And yet notwithstanding the inexcusableness of such transgressions, how ready our heavenly Father is to receive those that return to him, though after a long course of disobedience, and how willing to pardon their hainous and repeated provocations.

The parable that follows in the next chapter of the *rich man and*

---

[b] Luke xi. 11, &c.
[i] *Inter omnes Christi parabolas hæc sane eximia est, plena affectuum, & vividis picta coloribus.* Grot. ad v. 20.
[k] v. 17.

Laza-

Lazarus, represents to us with very affecting circumstances how apt a plentiful fortune is to benumb and stupify the soul, to shut out all serious consideration, to make men unmindful of the wants and necessities of their poor brethren, to regard nothing but the present gratification of their senses, and never *lift up their eyes* to heaven, till they see themselves surrounded with the flames of hell, and irreversibly doomed to take their portion in *that place of torment*.

The parable of the *king that would take an account of his servants* [g] offers powerful arguments to convince us of the great equity, and indeed necessity of forgiving others, in order to obtain forgiveness ourselves at the hands of God.

The parable of the *good Samaritan* [h] does very appositely shew

[g] Matth. xviii. 23, &c.
[h] Luke x. 30.

us that we ought to extend our kindness to all that stand in present need of our help, however differing from us in affections, persuasion, or interest.

The parable of the *rich man, who pleased himself with the prospect of living many years in wealth and jollity* [p], doth exactly represent the carnal security of wordly-minded men, and how terrible the message of death is to such persons, which very often cuts them off with a sudden stroke in the midst of their sins, and blasts all their fond hopes and vain expectations.

It would be too large an undertaking to give a particular account of all our Saviour's parables, and therefore I shall only just take notice of those which are put together in the xiiith chapter of St. *Matthew:* The first of which, the parable of the *Sower*, assigns the several reasons

[p] Luke xii. 16.

the HOLY SCRIPTURES. 209

which hinder men from receiving any benefit by the many sermons and instructions which they hear; and in those that follow, as also in many others, Christ in a prophetical manner describes the speedy growth and progress of the Christian Religion, and the state of the Church here upon earth unto the end of the world: In all which there are several mysterious admonitions, (not to be discovered but by a diligent searcher of the Scriptures) both instructing all ranks and orders of Christians in their several duties, and also warning the Church against those errors and corruptions, which should in process of time over-spread it. So that *Origen* [t] with great reason challenges *Celsus*, who despised the plainness of the Scriptures, to explain the parables of our Saviour, and unfold all those mysterious truths which are there couched under emblems and figures. And as our Saviour himself vouch-

[t] Orig. cont. Cels. *l.* 3. *p.* 122.

safed

safed to expound some of his parables to his disciples, apart from the multitude, so still there is need of a more intimate converse with the oracles of heaven, to enable us to discover all that spiritual wisdom which is there concealed under sensible representations.

II. The second thing observable in the Gospels, is our Saviour's *miracles*.

I shall not enter into a large discourse concerning the use of miracles, or the marks whereby we may distinguish true miracles from counterfeit ones. I shall only observe that our Saviour's *miracles* were not designed for ostentation, nor meerly to surprise men or gratify their curiosity, but to be really useful and beneficial to mankind; as if he intended thereby to instruct us, that all power ought to be employed to the doing of good, inasmuch as goodness is the most glorious and godlike quality of the divine nature, and that which

the HOLY SCRIPTURES. 211

gives a luftre to omnipotency itfelf [s]. Chrift's *miracles* made way for the reception of his doctrine, not only as they were a demonftration, that he who wrought them was a teacher fent from God, but likewife as they were an argument of our Saviour's own affectionate love and kindnefs to the fons of men, and a pledge and affurance of God's gracious purpofes towards them. When he gave fight to the blind, at the fame time he opened the eyes of their underftanding, that they might fee *the day-fpring from on high* that was come to *vifit them*. When he made the deaf to hear, fuch a work of mercy prepared them to receive with joy the glad tidings of the Gofpel. When he cleanfed the lepers, it was natural for thofe that were cured, to conclude that the fame perfon was able to purge them from the

---
[s] *Reddere Diis bonitatem, fine qua nulla majeftas eft.* Senec. Epift. 95.

pollution of their sins, and present them without spot to God. So suitable were all Christ's *miracles*, to the great design of his coming into the world, and disposed men to believe that he who was the healer of their bodily infirmities, was best qualified to be the physician of their souls.

And I think without perplexing ourselves with that nice enquiry, what are truly and properly miraculous works? or when must natural powers end, and supernatural begin? this may be sufficient determination of the question, concerning true and false *miracles,* that wherever any extraordinary work is wrought in a manner worthy of God, and beneficial to men, agreeing with fundamental truths formerly revealed, or confirming some new revelation of God's will, and promoting the great ends of piety and virtue in the world, these are certain marks of a true miracle, and we need no better evidence than this to distinguish God's messengers from impostors.

We

the HOLY SCRIPTURES. 213

We may further confider, that the prophets foretold [t] that the Meffias fhould come with *miracles*, and have inftanced in the principal kinds of miracles which he wrought. So that here we have God himfelf bearing witnefs by the mouth of his prophets to the truth of our Saviour's miracles, and guarding them from all fufpicion of impofture. And thus the miracles of our Lord did not only give teftimony to him, as they were wonderful works in themfelves, but likewife as they were an accomplifhment of fome of thofe predictions, which went before concerning him. And this muft needs be an undeniable argument for the truth of our Saviour's omiffion, to thofe that received the [u] writings of the prophets; and thofe that did not, by comparing thefe prophecies of the *Old Teftament*, with the events recorded in the *New*, might from hence

[t] *See* Ifa. xxxv. 5, 6.
[u] Matth. xi. 5. 6.

be

be fully convinced of the divine authority of both.

III. The third particular observable in our reading the Gospel is, *our Saviour's manner of life and conversation*; which was exactly agreeable to his doctrine and precepts.

St. *Luke* tells us [d] that the design of his Gospel was to give an account of all that Christ *both did and taught:* Implying that he practised first himself what he taught others, and laid no other burdens upon his disciples, but what he willingly underwent himself, and wherein he was their pattern as well as their director.

Humility and a patient submission to God's will; Charity, and a contempt to the world, are the peculiar doctrines of the Christian religion, and never were effectually recommended to the world till that appered; and our Saviour's life was one intire instance of these eminent virtues.

[d] Acts i. 1.

He made it his *meat and drink to do the will of him that sent him: He went about doing good,* and healing both the bodies and souls of men. He submitted to the lowest offices for the sake of others, and was at every body's service that desired his assistance. He condescended to the meanest company, that of Publicans and Sinners, when he had a prospect of doing any good upon them, and was content to lose the reputation of being a good man, that he might more effectually serve the ends of piety and goodness [e].

Never did so much goodness meet with such ungrateful and unsuitable returns; and yet this did not discourage him from going on as he had begun: He still continued unwearied in well-doing, endeavouring to conquer mens malice by kindness, and *overcome evil with good.*

[e] *Boni viri famam perdere, ne conscientiam perderet.* Senec.

He was the noblest instance of a sincere and unaffected contempt of the world that ever appeared in it. When he came into the world *he came unto his own*, as St. John speaks [f], he made it, and could easily have commanded all the glories and pleasures of it: Yet he *made himself of no reputation*, and took upon him so lowly a disguise, that when *he was in the world, though the world were made by him, yet it knew him not*. He chose to appear in such a mean condition, on purpose to *stain the pride of all worldly glory*, and to convince men that there were things of a quite different nature, namely, the favour of God and the unseen glories of the world to come, that did infinitely more deserve their esteem and regard. And he not only despised the glories of the world, but likewise patiently endured its affronts and reproaches; and when *he was reviled,*

[f] John i. 11.

not again; when he suffered he threatened not, but committed his cause to him that judges righteously [z]; to teach us by his behaviour in all conditions, to have an equal mind both in prosperity and adversity; to value that *honour which comes from God only*, and when we are unjustly dealt with, to comfort ourselves with the testimony of our conscience, and refer all to the righteous judgment of God.

This eminent example of a patient continuance in well doing, which appears so conspicuous in every part of our Saviour's life, is of great efficacy to persuade us *to go and do likewise*. It is commonly observed, that *Example is of greater force than bare precept*, because it sets forth the beauty of holiness to the life, and inflames men with a holy emulation of imitating those works, which appear so lovely and alluring. Precept

[z] 1 Pet. ii. 22.

indeed

indeed lays a higher obligation, and commands with greater authority; but example attracts more strongly, and hath a more powerful art of perſuaſion; in which reſpect we may juſtly ſay, that precept is but a *dead letter*, in compariſon of a *living example*. Eſpecially the example of our Saviour doth powerfully excite us to tread in his ſteps, ſince he, as the *captain of our ſalvation*, hath led the way, and if we follow him here, we ſhall aſſuredly reign with him hereafter.

IV. The fourth particular, very obſervable in our reading the Goſpels, is *the circumſtances of our Saviour's death*.

And here the virtues of humility, charity, and reſignation to God's will, which are the particular glories of Chriſt's life, appear ſtill more eminent and conſpicuous. In great humility *he took upon him the form of a ſervant*, and now he ſubmitted to a ſervile and ignominious death, and

was

was numbered among the transgressors. Out of his fervent charity he spent his life in the service of mankind, and now he laid it down to be a *ransom for many.* He gave the greatest demonstration of his charity, in dying even for his enemies, and offering up his blood, as well as his prayers, to procure a pardon for those that shed it. And received the traiterous kiss of *Judas* with such an unparallelled meekness, with such a gentle, and yet confounding, reproof, as was sufficient to melt down the malice of any one that was capable of repenting. And how tender his affections were towards his friends and followers, fully appears from his last discourses wherewith he took his leave of his disciples, recorded in the 13th, 14th, 15th, and 16th chapters of St. *John,* a portion of Scripture which we cannot too often read and consider, so full it is of excellent advice, and heavenly conso-

consolation. This we may call the *last sermon* of our dying Lord, which we ought to lay up in our minds, as the pledge of his love, and our own security. And when we feel any dejection of spirit, which the best of men sometimes labour under; how doth it revive our hearts, to hear him comforting his Disciples against their fears and sorrows, assuring them of his love and of God's favour, arming them with admirable instructions against the hour of temptation, and at last recommending them to God, in a most affectionate and fervent prayer, *chap.* xvii. the pattern of his intercession for us in heaven; and particularly praying for *Peter, that his faith might not fail*; and when afterward through fear he had denied his Master, recalling him to a sense of his duty by a gracious look, and by this first great instance of patience and long-suffering toward a believer, instructing us all not to despair of mercy,

the HOLY SCRIPTURES. 221

mercy, though we fall into sin after we have received the knowledge of the truth, but speedily to recover ourselves out of that evil state by a sincere repentance. And we may justly say, that the *Church* was *built* upon St. *Peter's repentance*, as well as upon the confession which he made of his *faith*. And when our Lord had in so an affectionate a manner performed all the tenderest offices of the kindest master, and the best friend, he absolutely resigned himself to the will of his father, and became *obedient to the death, even the death of the cross!* And when he had thus finished his course, we find him commending his soul to God in that his last ejaculation, *Father, into thy hands I commend my spirit*[1]*!*

Thus our Saviour hath given us an example how to live, and how to die; and if we follow this glorious

[1] Luke xxiii. 46.

pattern which he hath fet us, *neither death nor life will be able to feparate us from him.*

Thus I have taken a brief view of the moft remarkable occurrences in the Gofpels; a part of Scripture that does particularly recommend itfelf to our frequent reading and meditation, becaufe it is fo full of comfort and edification to all Chriftians, and withal fo admirably fitt d to the underftandings and capacities of the meaneft, as I have already obferved, [k] and will further appear if we confider in the

II. Place, the *manner of writing, made ufe of by the Evangelifts, their plainnefs of fpeech, and the other fignal marks of integrity, which are fo confpicuous in all the parts of the evangelical hiftory.*

Our Saviour fpoke with the plainnefs and majefty of a law-giver, not with the nicenefs or fubtilty of a phi-

[k] Chap iii.

losopher. He made it a greater part of his business *to preach the Gospel to the poor*, and in condescension to the meanest capacities used great plainness of speech. Accordingly the Evangelists related his discourses with the same plainness and simplicity of expression with which he spake to them, and recommended themselves and their writings by an unaffected manifestation of the truth, and not by the enticing words of art and sophistry. They recorded their own weaknesses and mistakes, as hath been already observed [b], and we cannot discover in their writings the least bias of passion or private interest, which is so visible in all human composures. The several Evangelists sometimes relate the same story with different circumstances; an undoubted argument of their sincerity, and a certain sign that the history which they relate is not a fable of

[b] Chap. ii.

their own contrivance. Men that have combined together to put a cheat upon the world, are naturally very apprehensive of being discovered, and to make all sure, take the utmost care that their evidence may agree in every point and tittle; but honest men need not be so scrupulous: And this unaccuracy of the Evangelists, if any one pleases so to stile it, may justly be ascribed to a particular direction of providence, because it shews that they were well assured, that their cause did not stand in need of the borrowed helps of exact method, studied expressions, and laboured periods.

I shall conclude this chapter with that weighty exhortation of the Apostle [a], *Take heed that ye despise not him that speaks* to you in the holy Gospels, *for if they escape not, who despised him that spake on earth, how*

[a] Heb. xii. 25.

shall we escape, if we turn away from him that speaks to us from Heaven? Nay, that came down from Heaven on purpose that he might speak unto us, and converse with us, and become both our teacher and our example.

CHAP.

CHAP. IX.

The principal matters to be observed in reading the Acts *and* Epistles *of the Apostles.*

OUR Saviour confined his preaching to *the lost sheep of the house of Israel**: But he chose his Apostles to be with him whilst he continued in the world, to be trained up under his discipline, and be witnesses of his life and doctrine, his death and resurrection. And when he was just departing out of the world he commanded them to testify what they had seen and heard, not only in *Judea* and the countries adjacent, but even *to the uttermost parts of the earth*ˢ.

A strange and improbable design, as it appears at first sight! that a few men of obscure birth and mean

---
* Matth. xv. 24.
ˢ Acts i. 8.

education, that had neither learning nor interest, should undertake to propagate a new religion in the world, that was in many points contrary to mens carnal inclinations and worldly interests; and persuade them to forsake the religion of their forefathers, which was not only deeply rooted in their minds, by custom and education, but also had all the external advantages of strength and interest which worldly power and policy could give it. No persons in their senses would have undertook such a design as this, unless they had been fully assured of a divine power that should assist them. And we can give no rational account of the wonderful success which accompanied their preaching, but that *he who was in them was greater than he that was in the world. God chose the weak things of the world, to confound the things that are mighty, that no flesh might glory in his presence* [q]; and the plant-

---

[q] 1 Cor. i. 29.

ing of the Gospel might appear to be the work of God, and not of man. And when the Christian Religion prevailed over all the strength and policy of the world, it was a demonstration that it came from God, because men could not overthrow it; and though they opposed it with their united force, yet they could not prevail against it, because God was with it. Therefore the Apostle deservedly reckons Christ being *preached among the Gentiles, and believed on in the world,* as part of the great *mystery of godliness,* and accounts it as wonderful a work as *God's being manifest in the flesh, and justified in the spirit* [e].

Now the doctrine which the Apostles preached to the persons who lived in their own time, they afterward by God's direction committed to writing, for the perpetual use of the Church in all ages. It was necessary that the Apostles should pro-

[e] 1 Tim. iii. 16.

vide

the HOLY SCRIPTURES. 229
vide for the inftruction of after-times as well as their own [t]; as they were the founders of the univerfal Church, which however enlarged by the acceffion of believers, or increafed in extent by the continuance of time, muft ftill be fupported by the fame foundation, that is, the doctrine which the Apoftles at firft delivered; and which fucceeding times could never have been certainly informed of, unlefs it had been committed to writing, the only fafe and fure way of conveying things down to pofterity. This doctrine is contained in the *Acts of the Apoftles*, written by St. *Luke*, and in the *Epiftles* directed to the feveral Churches, in order to confirm and build them up in that holy faith, wherein they had been inftructed.

[t] Διὰ τῆς τῶν Ἐπιστολῶν ἀρχῆς (Παῦλος) ὁ τοὺς τότε μόνον πιστοὺς, ἀλλὰ καὶ τοὺς ἐξ ἐκείνου μέχρι τῆς σήμερον γινομένους, καὶ τοὺς μέλλοντας δὲ ἔσεσθαι μέχρι τῆς ἐσχάτης τοῦ χριστοῦ παρουσίας, ὠφέλησέ τι καὶ ὠφελήσει, καὶ ὁ παύσεται, τοῦτο ποιῶν ἕως ἂν τὸ τῶν ἀνθρώπων διαμένῃ γένος. *Chryfoft.* l. 4. de *facerdotio* prope fin.

The

The usefulness of these holy writings I come now to consider: And shall first make some general observations concerning them: and then proceed to consider some of the principal matters to be regarded in our reading of them.

1. And first, I shall observe the agreement that is between those apostolical writings and the Gospel history, and how they mutually confirm and support each other.

The *Acts* relate several passages which confirm the truth of the Gospels, namely, the testimony which the Apostles gave to the life, doctrine, miracles, death, resurrection, and ascension of Christ, exactly agreeing with that account of each particular which we find in the Gospels; how they all of them joined in giving this testimony * and persisted in it, notwithstanding all the

* Acts ii. 32.

evils which either threatened them [c], as were actually inflicted upon them [d].

2. In the same book we find several promises which our Saviour made to his Disciples punctually performed: As that he would *endue them with power from on high, and enable them to be his witnesses among all nations* [e]: That they should work great and extraordinary miracles in his name [f]: That they should suffer many hardships for his sake, but that he would support them under their sufferings, and give them such wisdom, and presence of mind as should baffle and confound all their opposers [g].

3. The Epistles of the Apostles do likewise abundantly confirm all the considerable passages related in the Gospels and the Acts.

The particulars of our Saviour's life and death, are often referred to in them, as grounded upon the undoubted testimony of eye-witnesses,

[c] Chap. iv. 21. [d] Chap. v. 41. [e] Luke xxiv. 47, 49. [f] Mark xvi. 17, &c. John xiv. 12. [g] Matth. x. 17, &c. Luke xxi. 12, &c.

and

and being the foundation of the Chriftian Religion.

The fpeedy propagation of the Chriftian faith, recorded in the Acts, is confirmed beyond all contradiction, by innumerable paffages in the Epiftles written to the Churches already planted: And that within the compafs of the fame age wherein Chrift lived, when it had been the eafieft thing in the world to have difproved the matters of fact which the Apoftles attefted concerning him, if they had not been true.

The miraculous gifts which the Apoftles were endued with, and particularly the gift of tongues, are often appealed to in the fame writings, as an undeniable evidence of the divine miffion of the Apoftles. Particularly in the *firft Epiftle to the Corinthians* we may obferve fuch an evident proof that the gift of tongues was notoriously communicated to believers, as I think fhould be fufficient to fatisfy any unprejudiced man. We find, in the 12th and 14th chapters of that

Epi-

Epistle, the Apostle with great exactness distinguishes the several gifts of the Spirit [a], and gives directions for the orderly use and exercise of those gifts, particularly that of tongues [b], and corrects several abuses which were crept into the Church by a vain and unseasonable ostentation of that gift [c]. Now can any one suppose that a person in his right senses would make an elaborate discourse upon this argument, if there had been no such thing as the gift of tongues in the Church at that time? This would be to suppose the most absurd thing in the world, rather than believe the Scripture to be true.

I proceed now to consider the principal matters to be observed in our reading this part of the *New Testament* writings. And those are of three sorts.

---

[a] 1 Cor. xii. 8, 9, 10.   [b] Chap. xiv. 26, &c.
[c] Ibid. v. 6, &c.

1. The

1. *The doctrine contained in them;* as being an authentic commentary upon the Gospels, or a fuller explication of sundry articles of the Christian faith, which our Saviour had but sparingly spoke of in his own discourses.

2. *The exact idea these writings give us of the faith and manners of the first Christians:* A signal evidence of the divine power which accompanied the first preaching of the Gospel, and a noble pattern for us to imitate.

3. *The graces and virtues which appear so conspicuously in the apostolical writings, and prove the authors of them to be men sent from* God.

1. *In respect of the doctrine therein contained.* The doctrine which the Apostles taught their converts was the same in substance which Christ taught them, according to the tenor of Christ's commission to them, *Matth.* xxviii. 20. Yet the apostolical writings have this particular advantage, that they are a *divine and infallible commentary,* or an *authentic expli-*

explication of Christ's words in the Gospels, wherein the fundamentals of Christianity are admirably illustrated, and the mysterious parts of our holy faith more fully opened and explained, than they were by Christ himself [k]. He told his disciples whilst he was upon earth, [l] that *he had many things to say unto them, but they could not bear them* at the present, and therefore he referred them for fuller instructions in these matters, to the teaching of the Holy Ghost, which he promised to send down upon them after his departure.

To instance in some particulars of this kind.

1. There were some things which our Saviour did not fully and clearly explain to his disciples, but accommodated his expressions to those prejudices in which they had been

[k] Ὥσπερ χρισὸς εἰργάσατο μείζονα διὰ τῶν Μαθητῶν, ἢ δὶ ἰαυτῦ, ὅτω καὶ ἐφθέγξατο. Chrysost. Hom. *ult. in* Ep. *ad* Rom.
[l] John xvi. 12.

bred

bred up; as when he discourses concerning the nature and glories of his kingdom.

2. In other cases, though Christ spoke clearly and plainly, yet his Disciples did not apprehend his meaning at all, as namely, when he discourses concerning his own death and resurrection, and the redemption of the world, which was to be accomplished by that means.

3. Lastly, when our Saviour discourses concerning the calling of the *Gentiles*, he doth not express the thing in plain words, but only hints it in some general expressions, as when he says [m], *Many shall come from the east and west, and sit down with Abraham in the kingdom of heaven:* Or else obscurely intimates it in parables, particularly those *of the prodigal Son* [n], and of *the housholder that went out at the latter end of the*

---

[m] Matt. viii. 11.
[n] Luke xv. 11.

day to hire labourers into his vineyard º.

In all which cases, what the Apostles did not perfectly understand, they could not be supposed exactly to remember; but as the Holy Spirit *brought* our Saviour's words more distinctly to *their remembrance,* according to Christ's promise ᵖ, so by the direction of the same Spirit, they explained these great and important truths more fully than our Saviour did whilst he was upon earth; as will appear upon a brief view of what they say upon each of these heads.

To begin with the first, namely, *Our Saviour's discourses concerning the nature of his own kingdom.*

The *Jews* all along expected that the kingdom of Christ should *come with observation* ᑫ, that is, with the same pomp and splendor which accompanies an earthly monarchy,

º Matth. xx. 1.
ᵖ John xiv 26.
ᑫ Luke xvii. 20.

thereby

thereby to draw the eyes of the world after it. This is still the great stumbling-block of the *Jews*; and the most considerable objection they have against our Messias is, that *his kingdom is not of this world.* This opinion was so deeply rooted in the minds of the Apostles, that our Saviour did not think it proper to tear it up all at once, but rather to remove it by gentle and easy degrees. Accordingly, in compliance with their prejudices, we find him describing his kingdom, and the pre-eminence they were to enjoy in it, *by eating and drinking at his table, and sitting on thrones, and judging the twelve tribes of Israel*^e.

But after the Holy Ghost had given the Apostles clear and distinct apprehensions of the spiritual nature of Christ's kingdom, and wherein the happiness of it did consist, we find what noble representations they give

^e Luke xxii. 30. Matth. xix. 28.

us of the glories which are laid up for us in heaven, and what powerful arguments they take from hence to perſuade us not to ſet our minds upon the things of this world. They de-ſcribe the happineſs of the world to come, by an *inheritance incorruptible, undefiled, and that fadeth not away :* [f] by *a new heaven, and a new earth, wherein dwelleth righteouſneſs* [g], *where God ſhall be all in all :* [h] he ſhall reign with an abſolute dominion, and it ſhall be our honour and happineſs that God is exalted. They exhort us not to ſet our minds upon *the things that are ſeen and are temporal ; but on thoſe which are not ſeen, and are eternal* [i] *:* and by the continual exerciſe of faith and patience, of mortification and contempt of this world, to *make ourſelves meet to be partakers of the inheritance of the ſaints in light* [k].

[f] 1 Pet. i. 4. [g] 2 Pet. iii. 12. [h] 1 Cor. xv. 28. [i] 2 Cor. iv. 18. [k] Col. i. 12.

The same prejudice concerning the temporal glories of Christ's kingdom, made his disciples not understand the meaning of those several discourses of his concerning his sufferings, death, and resurrection [l]. The early conquests and triumphs of their master was what they dreamed of, and could not apprehend how he should become glorious thro' sufferings. Whereupon the doctrine of the cross, and the saving effects of it not being understood by the Apostles [m], till our Saviour had opened their understandings by his discourses upon this subject after his resurrection, we cannot expect so perfect an explication of that great and fundamental article of Christianity in the Gospels, as in the Epistles. In which, *Christ's dying for our sins, and and rising again for our justification*, is every where insisted upon as the

[l] *See* Mark ix. 10. Luke ix. 45. xviii. 34. [m] *See* Matth. xvi. 22.

the HOLY SCRIPTURES. 241

foundation of all our hopes: and the doctrine of the cross is there spoken of as a truth of such importance, that St. *Paul* [d], in comparison of it, despises all other sort of knowledge, whether divine or humane. From hence it is that the Apostles deduce those powerful motives to obedience, which are taken from the love, humility, and condescension of our Lord, and the right which he has to our service, having purchased us with the price of his blood [e]. From hence they derive those great obligations which lie upon Christians to exercise the duties of mortification and self-denial; of *crucifying the flesh with the affections and lusts* [k]: of patience under afflictions, and rejoicing in tribulations [l]: of being dead to this world, and *seeking those*

---

[d] 1 Cor. ii. 2. [e] *See* 1 Cor. vi. 20. 2 Cor. v. 15. 1 Gal. ii. 20. Tit. ii. 14. 1 Pet. i. 18, 19. [k] Gal. v. 24. vi. 14. Rom. vi. 6. 1 Pet. iv. 1, 2. [l] Phil. iii. 10. 2 Tim. ii. 11, 12. 1 Pet. ii. 19, &c. iv. 13.

L *things*

things which are above, where Christ sitteth at the right hand of God [m]. Thus as our Saviour *spoiled principalities and powers, and triumphed* over his enemies by the cross [n], so the good Christian overcomes the world by being crucified to it, and *becomes more than conqueror through Christ that loved him.*

The third instance which I gave of doctrines that may more fully be learned from the Epistles and other writings of the Apostles, than from the words of Christ recorded in the Gospels, was *the calling of the Gentiles to make one and the same Church with the Jews.*

The many prophecies of the *Old Testament* which foretel the calling of the *Gentiles*, were sufficient to convince the *Jews* that in the times of the Messias, God would reveal the knowledge of himself, and his will to the world more fully than ever

---

[m] Coloss. iii. 1. &c.   [n] Chap. ii. 15.

he had done before. But the extraordinary value which they had for themselves, and the privileges which they fancied were peculiar to their own nation, made them unwilling to believe that the Gentiles should ever be *fellow heirs* with the *Jews of the same body* or Church with them, and *partakers of the* same *promises in Christ by the Gospel* [n]. This St. *Peter* himself could hardly be persuaded to believe, till he was convinced by a particular vision vouchsafed to him for that purpose [o]. And St. *Paul* tells us that this was a mystery which was but newly revealed *to the Apostles by the Spirit* [p]: and therefore not fully discovered by Christ before.

And here it is proper to observe to what excellent purposes the Apostles improve this new Revelation which was vouchsafed to them: how they

[n] Ephes. iii. 6.
[o] Acts x. 28.
[p] Eph. iii. 5.

take occasion from hence in their writings to magnify the riches of God's grace, *in making his ways known upon earth*, and bringing men *out of darkness into his marvellous light*: how they set forth the divine power which accompanied the preaching of the Apostles, whereby they that were *sometimes foolish, disobedient, and serving divers lusts and pleasures* [b] *were washed, were justified in the name of the Lord Jesus* [c], and learned to *put off the old man which was corrupt according to the deceitful lusts: and to be renewed in the spirit of their mind* [d]. Lastly, from hence they powerfully exhort us *Gentiles,* now we *have the light to walk as children of the light* [e], *and to walk worthy of that holy calling wherewith we are called* [f]: Always remembring that we were not *redeemed from our vain conversation with sil-*

---

[b] Tit. iii. 3. [c] 1 Cor. vi. 11. [d] Eph. iv. 24.
[e] Eph. v. 8. [f] Chap. iv. 1.

ver and gold, but with the precious blood of the Son of God [f].

I shall conclude my remarks concerning the doctrinal parts of the *Epistles*, with one general observation; namely, That although most of them were writ upon particular occasions, and with relation to the present exigencies of the Churches,to which they are directed, yet you may find the Apostles take occasion from every hint that is offered to them, to explain the mysteries of the Gospel, to set forth the excellency of it, to persuade men to live up to the height of its precepts. They descend to give particular directions for discharging the duties relating to all states and conditions of life; those of princes and subjects [g]; of pastors and people [h], of husbands and wives [i], of parents and children [k].

[f] 1 Pet. i. 18, 19. [g] Rom. xiii. 1 Pet. ii. 13, &c. [h] *In the Epist. to* Tim. *and* Titus. *See also* 1 Thess. v. 12, 13, *and* Heb. xiii. 7, 17. [i] Eph. v. 22, &c. Coloss. iii. 18, &c. 1 Pet. iii. 1, &c. [k] Eph. vi. 1, &c. Coloss. iii. 20, 21.

of masters and servants [1]. This is a convincing argument that the holy Spirit which influenced their pens, had not only an eye to the particular exigencies of the Christians, who lived in those times, but likewise directed the holy writers to enlarge themselves upon such points of doctrine and practice, which were of universal concern, and would be for the benefit of the faithful in all succeeding generations. I proceed to consider,

II. *The exact idea which those apostolical writings give us of the faith and manners of the first Christians:* A signal evidence of the divine power which accompanied the first preaching of the Gospel, and a noble pattern for us to imitate.

Amidst those numerous sects which divide the Christian Church, the sober men of all parties seem to agree

---

[1] Eph. vi. 5, &c. Col. iii. 22, &c. Tit. ii. 9. 1 Pet. ii. 18.

the HOLY SCRIPTURES. 247

in this, that the true model and pattern of the Chriſtian Religion, with reſpect to faith and manners, is to be taken from the doctrine and practice of the apoſtolical Church. And without meddling at preſent with doctrinal points, (as being more ſubject to diſpute and controverſy) if we take a view of the manners and behaviour of the primitive Chriſtians, as they are deſcribed in the *Acts* and the *Epiſtles*, we may draw ſuch a portraiture of that firſt and pureſt Church, as will at once raviſh us with delight and admiration at the ſight of its beauties and perfections, and ſtrike us with ſhame and confuſion, when we find how much we are degenerated from the virtues of our fore-fathers. It is therefore very proper frequently to repreſent to ourſelves and others the *pattern* and *faſhion* of this *houſe of God*, as it is delineated by the *maſter-builders* thereof, *that we may all be aſhamed of what we have done, and*

L 4 *of*

of our iniquities and deviations from it [o].

We cannot look upon those writings but we shall every where discover with what joy and gladness, with what reverence and attention, the first converts received the Gospel, *not as the word of men, but as it was indeed the word of God* [p], *and the power of God unto salvation*: How highly they esteemed the ministers and preachers of this word, and *received them as messengers, or angels of God, and even as Christ Jesus* [q], in whose name they spake. From the same holy writings we may learn, how much their thoughts were fixed upon heavenly things; in the midst of their employments meditating upon God's word, and celebrating his praises [r]: being careful to perform their private Devotions, at those solemn hours of

[o] Ezek. xliii. 10, 11. [p] 1 Thes. ii. 13. [q] Galat. iv. 14. [r] Eph. v. 19. Colos. iii. 16. James v. 13.

the HOLY SCRIPTURES. 249

Prayer [t], which pious men in former times [u] had set apart for that purpose: And laying hold of all opportunities of joining in the public worship of God, *in season and out of season,* early in the morning [w], and late at night [x], according as they could assemble with the greatest security: And when any public calamity threatened them, imploring the aid of Heaven without ceasing, and *continuing instant in Prayers and Supplications night and day* [z]:

The same Scriptures do abundantly declare how ready the first Christians were, to do or suffer any thing that might promote the glory of God, and testify the sincerity of their obedience to his laws; doing good with an unwearied diligence [b], and

---

[t] *See* Acts ii. 15. iii. 1. x. 9. xvi. 25. 1 Thes. v. 19. [u] *See* Psalm lv. 17. Dan. vi. 10. [w] *See* Acts xii. 12. & Plin. Epist. l. 10. Ep. 97. Tertull. Apolog. cap. 39. [x] Acts xx. 7. [z] Chap. xii. 5. [b] *See* Phil. i. 3, &c. Colos. i. 3, &c. 1. Thes. i. 3. 2 Thes. i. 3.

L 5 endu-

enduring evil, not only patiently, but joyfully ᵉ. What unfeigned love they shewed toward all their brethren ᶠ, and with what a fervent charity, *even beyond their power*, they relieved the necessities of those that were in want ᵍ. How sober and regular they were in their private deportment ʰ, using the things of the world as those that looked upon themselves to *be strangers here*, and denizens of the heavenly city ⁱ.

The apostolical writings afford us two undeniable proofs of the unblameable lives of the first Christians. The first is, that the Apostles there glory in the lives of their Disciples, as a convincing argument of the divine grace which accompanied their

---

ᵉ 2 Thes. v. 4. Heb x. 34. Acts xiii. 52.
ᶠ Eph. i. 15. 1 Thes. iv. 10. Heb. xiii. 1.
1 Pet. i. 22. ᵍ Acts xi. 29. Rom. xv. 26.
1 Cor. xvi. 1. 2 Cor. viii. 2, 3. Philem.
ver. 7. 3 John. vi. ʰ 1 Thes. iv. 1. 1 Pet.
iv. 4. ⁱ Ἡμῶν πολίτευμα ἐν οὐρανοῖς ὑπάρχει, Phil. iii. 20.

conversion [k], an argument we are forced now to decline: And in the next place, that whosoever among them was guilty of any scandalous behaviour, had a mark presently set upon him [l]: his acquaintance first avoided his conversation, and then the Church turned him out of their Communion, as a person unworthy of that holy society [m]. They did not prostitute Church-censures to base and secular ends, which has made them lose all their authority in these latter ages, but they inflicted them *for edification and not for destruction* [n], with a hearty concern for the honour of God and the souls of men, with all the signs of mourning and sor-

[k] 1 Cor. vi 11. Phil. ii. 15, 16. 1 Thes. iii. 19, 20. 2 Thes. i. 4. Colos. i. 6. 1 John ii. 14.
[l] *Idem de sua ætate testantur, Justin. M. Apol. II. rectius l. n. 17. & 20. Edit. Oxon. & Lactant. Divin. Instit. b. 3. c. 25. Tertull. Apolog. cap. 3.*
[m] 1 Cor. v. 11, 13. 2 Thes. iii. 6, 14.
[n] 2 Cor. xiii. 10.

row [*], for him who had incurred them, as one who by his sins had provoked God, had endangered his own salvation, and had dishonoured that *worthy name whereby he was called*. So offensive was a single blemish in that Church, which endeavoured to keep itself without spot or wrinkle, and fit to be the spouse of the immaculate Lamb.

This short view of the state of the apostolical Church, is of itself sufficient to satisfy any considering man of the truth of that holy religion, which then first appeared in the world. For we find the Apostles often appealing to the experience of their converts, for the truth of what they say concerning the divine power, which accompanied their preaching: And it appears that those first Christians, who could with the greatest ease trace their religion to its original, were most fully convinced of the

---

[*] *See* 1 Cor. v. 2. 2 Cor. vii. 11, 12, 21.

truth

truth of it, lived up to the height of its principles, and sealed it with their death and sufferings.

III. A third thing very observable in the apostolical writings, is, *The graces and virtues of the authors of them, which appear there so conspicuously, and prove the persons endued with such extraordinary qualities, to be men sent from God:* Out of the abundance of the heart the mouth speaketh [e], as our Saviour observes. Speech is one of the surest indications of mens inward dispositions. Indeed, hypocrites do often shew great zeal and religion, and pretend to all the heights and raptures of an inflamed devotion: But they cannot act a part so cunningly, but that the vizard will at some time or other drop off unawares, and they will discover a great deal of spiritual pride, or secular ambition lurking under the specious shew of religion and

[e] Matth. xii. 34.

godli-

godlineſs. But the writings of the Apoſtles have all the air of an unaffected piety, and untainted integrity that can be imagined; *As of ſincerity, as of God, in the ſight of God ſpeak they in Chriſt* [d]; they ſpeak as thoſe that believed themſelves, and were thoroughly convinced of the truth and great importance of the things they deliver.

We cannot look into the hiſtory of their *Acts* or their *Epiſtles*, but we may every where obſerve remarkable inſtances of their conſtancy and patience in ſuffering for the teſtimony of the Goſpel; of their unwearied labours in publiſhing it; of their hearty concern for the good ſucceſs of their miniſtry; of their renouncing all ſelf-intereſt and worldly conſiderations, and ſeeking nothing but the honour of God, and the good of mens ſouls. There is ſet before our eyes their *work of faith, their labour of love, their pa-*

[d] 2 Cor. ii. 17.

tience

the HOLY SCRIPTURES. 255
tience of hope, their unaffected contempt of the world, their zeal for the advancement of Chrift's kingdom, and in general how they make it their chief aim to approve themſelves to God, *To finiſh their courſe with joy, and faithfully to diſcharge the miniſtry they had received from the Lord Jeſus.* Theſe characters carry their own evidence along with them, and are of far greater force than all the *enticing words of man's wiſdom.* They are a demonſtration of that holy Spirit which influenced the ſpeakers, and muſt needs ſink deep into the minds of all attentive hearers.

But it may not be amiſs to take a more particular view of the virtues and graces which appear ſo eminently in the writings of the Apoſtles.

And *firſt* we will conſider the evident marks we find there *of their ſincere piety towards God.*

Nothing

Nothing but a hearty sense of their duty to God, and a desire to approve themselves to him, could have engaged them in so difficult an undertaking as that of publishing the Gospel, and standing up in the defence and confirmation of it, *when it was every where spoken against*. A great part of the world *became their enemies, because they told them that truth*, which they had no mind to hear, and had not so much civility as to thank them for their good intentions, and to take the good advice, which they offered, kindly at their hands. Our Saviour forewarned them, that *in the world they must expect tribulation* *, and the event justified the truth of the prediction. So that they could have no reasonable inducement to undertake a work attended with so much trouble and difficulty, but only a hearty zeal for the glory of God,

* John. xvi. 33.

the HOLY SCRIPTURES. 257
whose they were [f], *and whom they served in the Gospel of his Son* [g]. *As we were allowed of God to be put in trust with the Gospel,* faith St. *Paul, so we speak not as pleasing men, but God, who searcheth the hearts* [h].

Secondly, the *Apostles* charity to the souls of men, and their hearty concern for their salvation, does in the next place offer itself to our consideration.

They had no greater joy than to hear that their children in Christ *walked in the truth,* as St. *John* testifies [i]. *Now we live,* faith St. *Paul* to the *Thessalonians, if we stand fast in the Lord* [k]. In like manner, nothing affected them with so much grief and sadness, as when they understood that any of their converts had brought a scandal upon his holy profession by his evil behaviour. *Who*

[f] Acts xxvii. 23.   [g] Rom. i. 9.   [h] 1 Thes.
ii. 4.   [i] 3 John iv.   [k] 1 Thes. iii. 8.   *See*
chap. ii. 19, 20.

is weak, faith the Apoſtle, *and I am not weak, who is offended, and I burn not* [1]*?* *That which comes upon me daily,* adds he in the ſame place, *is the care of all the Churches,* and my concern for their ſpiritual welfare. This made him ſo diligent to avoid giving any occaſion of offence, leſt the miniſtry itſelf ſhould be blamed for his ſake [m] : This made him *preach the Goſpel freely* [n], and wave that right which he had of demanding maintenance from thoſe to whom he preached it, and choſe to *ſuffer* any hardſhips, rather than *hinder the Goſpel of Chriſt,* or ſtop the progreſs of it [o] ; This made him not only labour without ceaſing in the work of the Goſpel, *that by all means he might ſave ſome ;* but likewiſe rejoice in his ſufferings for the ſake of it,

---

[1] 2 Cor. xi. 28, 29.
[m] 2 Cor. vi. 3.
[n] 2 Cor. xi. 7.
[o] 1 Cor. ix. 12, 13, 14. *See* 1 Theſ. ii. 6, 7, 8, 9.

when

the HOLY SCRIPTURES. 259
when he found that they were serviceable to so noble an end, as that of the salvation of men. *I endure all things,* saith he, *for the Elect's sake, that they may obtain the salvation which is in Christ Jesus, with eternal glory* ᵉ. And no wonder that his charity was so fervent toward his Converts, *his children in Christ*, as he often stiles them ᶠ, when he could find in his heart to be *accursed from Christ* ᵍ for the sake of the *Jews* his fleshly brethren. Such an expression of charity as we scarce dare venture to interpret, and as much exceeds our comprehension as it is above our imitation! If we would give an exact idea of an evangelical pastor, and the concern he ought to have for the souls committed to his charge, we cannot do it in more significant words than those of St.

ᵉ 2 Tim. ii. 9.
ᶠ 1 Cor. iv. 15. Gal. iv. 19. Philem. ver. 10.
ᵍ Rom. ix. 3.

Paul

Paul in the *second Epistle* to the *Corinthians*, chap. vi. from the beginning to the eleventh verse: And in the *first Epistle* to the *Thessalonians*, chap. ii. from verse 1, to 14, both which places contain a description of his own and the rest of the Apostles behaviour in that weighty office, and are a pattern for all that shall succeed them in that employment.

Thirdly, Let us take a short view of the Apostles *sincere and unaffected contempt of the world,* as it appears every where in their writings.

Indeed they met with so much hard usage in the discharge of their office, as would have discouraged any men that had the least regard for the honours, the profits, or the pleasures of the world: But their minds were above such low considerations. Hear St. *Paul*'s attestation for himself and his brethren [h]:

[h] 1 Thes. ii. 3, 5, 6.

Our

Our exhortation was not of deceit, nor of uncleanness, nor in guile; neither at any time used we flattering words, as ye know, nor a cloak of covetousness, God is witness: nor of men sought we glory. When the men of *Lycaonia* would have offered sacrifice to him and *Barnabas*, we find them renting their cloaths with the greatest indignation, and crying out[1], *Sirs! Why do ye these things? We are men of like passions and infirmities with yourselves.*

It is confessed, that there have been those who have sacrificed their ease, interest, and even life itself, to vain glory: But if we suppose this to have been the ruling principle in the minds of the Apostles, it was certainly the most unaccountable vanity that ever was heard of, and such as acted most in contradiction to itself. For they that were supposed to be governed by it, voluntarily chose po-

[1] Acts xiv. 15.

verty, reproach and sufferings, things which naturally bring contempt upon men in the eyes of the world, (and which none, if in their senses, can make matter of choice, but upon a principle of conscience) and at the same time disclaimed all worth and merit in themselves, and took all occasions to magnify the grace of God bestowed upon such great sinners as they profess themselves to be.

 The chief design of all their writings is to exalt God, and to humble man: They often express their desire, that *in all things God may be glorified*, from whom they acknowledge *every good and perfect gift to proceed*, and to whom they judge it most fit, that all honour and praise should be returned.

 Lastly, I shall briefly consider *that constancy and patience in suffering for the truth's sake*, of which there are so many eminent instances in the writings of the Apostles.

Not

Not to mention any more particulars, which every one's reading may suggest to him, let us hear the catalogue which St. *Paul* gives us of the persecutions he endured [k] : *In labours more abundant, in stripes above measure, in prisons more frequent, in deaths oft. Of the Jews five times received I forty stripes, save one: Thrice was I beaten with rods, once was I stoned: Thrice I suffered shipwreck, and a night and a day I have been in the deep. In journeying often, in perils of waters, in perils of robbers, in perils by my own countrymen, in perils by the heathen, in perils in the city, in perils in the wilderness, in perils in the sea, in perils among false brethren. In weariness and painfulness, in watchings often, in hunger and thirst, in fastings often, in cold and nakedness.*

Nothing could have supported men under such continual hardships and

[k] 2 Cor. xi. 23, &c.

dangers, but a good cause and a good conscience; and these two comforts made them endure afflictions not only patiently, but joyfully. And there cannot be a more convincing argument either of mens sincerity, or of the divine assistance attending them, than to see persons of a cool reason and settled judgment, triumph over the fears of death, and lay down their lives in testimony unto the truth.

Thus I have briefly surveyed those eminent characters of piety and virtue, which so signally appear in the writings of the Apostles, and are both an evident proof of that divine spirit which influenced their pens, and a glorious pattern for us to imitate. The instances I have pitched upon, are chiefly taken out of the Epistles of St. *Paul*. But because it may be pretended that he had the assistance of human learning, whereby his mind was enlarged and improved, we will take a short view of the

the HOLY SCRIPTURES. 265
the writings of the other Apoſtles, who cannot be ſaid to have had the advantages of a learned education. And here it is eaſy to obſerve what an affectionate ſtrain of piety runs thro' the Epiſtles of St. *Peter*, how much edification and inſtruction is conveyed to us in the humble plainneſs of St. *James*. But that which more eſpecially offers itſelf to our admiration, is that noble ſimplicity of ſtile and expreſſion, which is ſo remarkable in the writings of St. *John*. With what a native grandeur and majeſty does he ſet forth the moſt elevated thoughts and ſublimeſt myſteries, in plain and inartificial words [a]? God, who diſtributes his graces and gifts ſeverally as he pleaſes, ſeems to have given to St. *John* a peculiar inſight into the myſteries of the divine love. He was Chriſt's beloved Diſciple; he lay in his boſom;

[a] *See the beginning of his Goſpel and firſt Epiſtle.*

M from

from whence the love of God was transfused, and as it were breathed into his holy breast. His soul was touched with a deep and lively sense of it: His thoughts were big with that noble argument: He takes a particular delight in enlarging upon it, and he treats of it in a plain and inartificial stile; but yet with such a lofty eloquence, as is above the rules of human art, and can only be ascribed to the influence of that holy Spirit which gave him utterance.

Hos cum legimus, quem philosophum non contemnimus? How dry and insipid are the witty sayings, and the studied periods of the philosophers, when compared with the *words of eternal life,* which these holy men spake? The foundation of the religion which they preach, is solid, and not to be shaken; they deliver nothing upon that subject, but what they have seen and heard: (and matters of fact are not so easily attacked by by sophistry, as points of speculation.) The arguments they propound to convince men, are firm and solid: The motives they use to persuade them, are weighty and powerful; the best understandings must yield to the strength of them, and the meanest are capable of apprehending the force of them. And how must the heart of every attentive reader *burn within him,* when he sees these holy writers unfold the mysteries of the Gospel, and discover the whole counsel of God, not *in the words which man's wisdom teacheth, but which the Holy Ghost teacheth?* Who can forbear crying out, *From whence have these men such* mighty gifts, and *what wisdom is this that is given to them,* that unlearned and ignorant men should confound *the wisdom of the wise,* and baffle the subtilty of *the disputers of this world* [1]?

---

[1] Ουδὲν ἀμαθέστερον Πέτρου, ἐδὲν ἰδιωτικώτερον Παύλου, ἀλλ' ὅμως ὁ ἰδιώτης οὗτος, καὶ ὁ ἀμαθὴς ἐκεῖνος, μυ-

To conclude this chapter: The virtues and graces which shine forth in every part of the apostolical writings, are alone a demonstration that the doctrine which they taught came from God, the fountain of truth and holiness: For certainly the Father of lies would never pitch upon such persons to carry on a contrivance of fraud and falshood. *Either make the tree good, and its fruit good; or else make the tree corrupt, and its fruit corrupt; for the tree is known by it's fruit* [m] : As our Saviour unanswerably argues. And as St. *Paul* reasons to the same purpose [n], *What fellowship can righteousness have with unrighteousness; or what Communion can light have with darkness?* As little concord hath *Christ with Belial.* And to say that Persons of such holiness and integrity as himself and

μυρίες ἐνίκησαν Φιλοσόφες, μυρίες ἐπεςόμισαν ῥήτορας. Chrysost. *Præfat. in* Ep. *ad* Rom.
[m] Matth xii. 33.
[n] 2 Cor. vi. 14.

his Apoſtles undeniably appear to have been, ſhould either make or advance a lie, is to ſuppoſe one of theſe two things; either that God Almighty ſhould be aſſiſting in ſetting up the Devil's kingdom, or that Satan ſhould join a helping hand to pull down his own.

CHAP. X.

The Advantages *of Revelation* above *natural Light*, or any *Syſtem of the Law of Nature.*

Although we have juſt reaſon to prefer revelation before the bare light of nature, as may eaſily appear from what has been hitherto obſerved, and from a great deal more that might be added upon ſo copious a ſubject; yet I would not have any thing I have ſaid miſconſtrued, as if it were ſpoken in derogation to natural religion. For I readily acknowledge, that all revelation ſuppoſes the truth of the principles of natural religion, and nothing is to be received as ſuch, which evidently contradicts or overthrows thoſe principles. So we are to look upon natural religion, as the foundation, and revelation as the ſuperſtructure, that which adds

the

the last and finishing stroke to the whole work.

And in my judgment this one consideration is sufficient to recommend the Scripture Revelation to every impartial reader, *viz.* That it not only supposes and builds upon the received principles of natural religion, concerning the being and providence of God, and the rewards and punishments of a future state, but likewise improves and enforces them, by placing them in a better light, and giving us greater evidence for them, than bare reason could suggest.

But alas! there are too many now-a-days that fancy God might have saved all this trouble, that revelation is a clog to religion instead of a help: They are of opinion that the law of nature is a sufficient rule for practice, and the intimations of another life; and the general notices of God's mercy, which reason offers to us, are as good a security for men's salvation as they need desire. Thus do ungrate-

ungrateful men requite God for his mercies; and this is all the return they think fit to make to him for those wonderful expressions of his love, *in sending his Son into the world, that we might live through him.*

To convince men of their folly, as well as their ingratitude, I shall briefly consider the *great advantages of revelation above the bare light of nature, or any system of natural religion*; and that upon three accounts.

1. Because *revelation explains our duty more fully and distinctly.*

2. *It enforces it by a more commanding authority.*

3. The *arguments it makes use of to that purpose, are more powerful and persuasive*; and likewise *more popular and better suited to common capacities.*

1. *Revelation explains our duty more fully and distinctly*; that is, it gives us a more distinct account of the several branches of our duty, and

and explains the due extent of each particular branch.

There is no queſtion, but the *laws of nature* are God's laws, who is the author of nature, and that their obligation is enforced upon men by natural ſanctions; but yet the authority of each particular branch of them is not ſo clear and indiſputable, as to be obvious to every capacity. And this uncertainty gives a pretence to men to judge for themſelves, how far the obligation of natural duty extends, and no doubt but they will find out ſome favourable exception for their own darling luſts and vices. Upon this account, conſidering the great degeneracy of the world, the law of nature is too uncertain a rule for men to ſquare their lives by. And indeed here lies that *myſtery of iniquity*, which is now working under the pretence of *Deiſm*, or the maintaining natural religion in oppoſition to revelation; *viz.* that men would fain have a religion of their own making,

making, and be obliged by the laws of God no farther than they like them. So that there is absolute need of a superior authority to over-rule the cavilling wits of men [m], and silence those objections which mens lusts will be industrious to raise against such parts of their duty, which they are unwilling to be restrained by. And since eternal life is the free gift of God, it must needs be the most certain and satisfactory way for God himself to declare his mind concerning it, and the means whereby it may be obtained.

" If we be sent to read the laws
" of nature in the tables of our own
" hearts, saith our excellent bishop
" *Taylor* [n] where some things are
" disordered by passion, many more
" are written by interest; some are
" indited by custom, and others

---

[m] *Decemur non infinitis conversationumque plenis disputationibus, sed authoritate Legum domitas habere libidines*, &c. Cic. de Orat. lib. 1.

[n] *Duct. dubitant.* l. 2. c. 2. Rule 7. n. 15, &c.

" im-

"imprinted by education; and a-
"mongst several men these are the
"authors of contrary inscriptions:
"I say, if we have no better direc-
"tor than this, whereby to square
"our actions, we shall find ourselves
"at a loss for the managing our be-
"haviour in some of the weightiest
"concerns of life."

They that contend for the sufficiency of natural religion in opposition to revelation, or the written word of God, do not consider how much revelation hath contributed to clear up mens minds, and give them more distinct apprehensions of natural truths than the world had before. When a new discovery is made, we find most people flatter themselves so far, as to fancy that they could have hit upon the very same thing, if they had but given their minds to it. The same prejudice lies in the case before us: The word of God hath placed the principles of natural religion in their true light; and when truth is once made plain and evident, it seems to be so easy and obvious, that every body fancies he knew as much before. But whoever considers how much the wisest and best philosophers were at a loss when they undertook to settle the great foundations of religion, and the principal branches of moral duty, may be easily convinced, that reason is but a blind guide in heavenly things, even to those who had made the best improvement of their natural talent.

I shall illustrate this matter by instancing in a few particulars.

The laws of *purity of heart*, of *loving our enemies*, and *overcoming evil with good*; these and several other sublime duties are expresly commanded, and if I may so speak, *enacted* under the Gospel. But although most of them have been recommended as highly reasonable by the wisest heathens, yet they never could obtain the force and estimation of of laws in the world, until the word of God re-inforced their obligation. Which one confideration is an undeniable proof that the corruption of human nature, and that degeneracy of manners which overfpread the world before the times of the Gofpel, had fo far obfcured the laws of nature, that there was need of teachers fent from God to inftruct mankind in fome parts of their duty, which might indeed have been difcovered by the light of reafon, when it was in its primitive perfection, but was in a great meafure defaced and obliterated by falfe principles and corrupt cuftoms.

St. *Paul* fpeaking of himfelf, whilft he was under the *Jewifh* difpenfation, tells us [*], that *he had not known luft to be a fin, unlefs the law had faid,* in exprefs words, *thou fhalt not covet.* Without doubt, if he had narrowly confulted his own reafon, that would

[*] Rom. vii. 7.

have informed him, that we ought to obey God with the whole man, and are bound to ferve him with all the faculties both of our foul and body; and confequently that the irregular motions of the mind and thoughts were properly fins, as being breaches of that intire obedience which is due to God Almighty. But the Apoſtle's meaning is this, that his own natural corruption, joined with the prejudices of his education, which was among the *Phariſees* [r], and confirmed by the falſe notions of good and evil, which ran current in the world, had ſo far blinded his judgment, as to make him overlook ſo conſiderable a part of his duty, and nothing but the expreſs commands of the law could have rectified his miſtake in this matter.

And if the law of *Moſes* were ſo very inſtrumental in clearing up the

---

[r] Τὸ μηκέτι ποιῆσαι ἔργον Βελυσάμενος ἐκ ἔςι τιμωρίας ἄξιον, inquit *Joſephus* de *Antiocho*, Antiq. l. 12. c. 13.

due

due meaning and extent of the law of nature, certainly the laws of Chrift are much more ufeful to that purpofe; fo that both together may juftly be efteemed the moft perfect rule of life the world was ever yet acquainted with, and abundantly fufficient to render us *thoroughly furnifhed unto every good work.*

2. A fecond advantage which revelation hath above the unwritten law of nature, is, that it *fpeaks to us with a more commanding authority.* The law of reafon is indeed the voice of God within us. But yet it is but a *ftill fmall voice,* and fuch as is fcarce heeded, but by a liftening and attentive ear: nor is it of fufficient authority to reform mankind, confidering with how much violence mens lufts and paffions make head againft it. Reafon can exercife but a feeble authority over fuch rebellious fubjects; it can only admonifh them, as old *Eli* did his profligate Sons, and fay to them, *why do ye fuch things?*

things? *It is no good report that I hear of you:* and in both cases you shall find the reproof to be equally despised.

How faint are the reproofs of philosophers, when applied to the correction of obstinate offenders? to tell such persons that they act in contradiction to their reason, and below the dignity of their nature, is to make them accountable only to themselves, and they will easily find ways to discharge themselves from such feeble obligations. What sinner would not rather part with a fine notion, than deny himself the satisfaction of his lusts and pleasures? It is in vain to think to reform the world by any rules or precepts, but such as are enforced by the authority of God, that *supreme law-giver, who is able both to save and to destroy;* who hath the power of eternal life and death in his hands, and can make the most daring sinner tremble at his word.

^d Ac-

[d] Accordingly our Saviour, who was *the brightnefs of his Father's glory, and the exprefs image of his perfon, fpake with authority,* as his hearers themfelves confeffed [e]. He delivered his precepts with the plainnefs and majefty of a lawgiver, not with the nicenefs and fubtilty of a philofopher. His *words were fpirit, and they were life;* they pierced into the foul and confcience, and laid open the innermoft receffes of the heart; and in his difcourfes we find the majefty of a God, joined with the gentlenefs of a friend, and the kindnefs of a brother.

In like manner if we confult the writings of the Apoftles, with what authority do they teach? With what majefty do they command? With what feverity do they rebuke? With

---

[d] *Quanta eft prudentia hominis ad demonftrandum bonum, quanta authoritas ad exigendum: tam illa falli facilis, quàm ifta contemni.* Tertull. Apol. c. 45. [e] Matth. vii. 29.

what tender concern do they chastise? and with what weighty arguments do they persuade all Christians *to adorn the doctrine of God their Saviour in all things.*

3. A third advantage which Revelation hath above the light of nature, consists in this, *that the arguments it makes use of to explain and enforce our duty, are more powerful and persuasive, and withal more popular, and better suited to common capacities.*

Our Saviour by taking our nature upon him, hath brought heaven down to us, and given us an assurance of its promises in such a way as lies most level to our capacities, and works most forcibly upon our affections. The revealing the deep things of God in such a familiar and sensible manner as the Gospel does, carries a mighty and convincing evidence along with it, as St. *John* sets forth in very emphatical expressions, at the beginning of his first *epistle, That which was from the beginning, which we have*

the HOLY SCRIPTURES. 283
have heard, which we have seen with our eyes, which we have looked upon, and our hands have handled of the word of life: for the life was manifested, and we have seen it, and bear witness, and shew unto you that eternal life which was with the Father, and was manifested unto us. That which we have seen and heard, declare we unto you.

If we will allow the principles of natural Religion all the force and evidence they can reasonably be desired, yet it is certain they are but of little use to persons of ordinary capacities [g], who before the Revelation of the Gospel, were rather governed by the general instincts of natural conscience, and the authority of human laws and customs, than by the dictates of reason methodically deduced from clear and self-evident principles. The arguments which philosophers made use of to prove the immortality of the soul,

[g] *See* 1 Cor. i. 21.

and

and a future state, were too nice and metaphysical to be apprehended by the vulgar understandings: And in order to make our perfect system of the laws of nature, men must attend to a long train of propositions, and be able to discover how one depends upon another.

Whereas in the holy Writings, instead of the uncertain dictates of a natural law, too often obscured by passion, and depraved by ill custom, we have the Will of God made known to us by his Son, *who was in the bosom of his Father*, intimately acquainted with all his counsels and purposes, and was pleased to come down from heaven, that he might shew us the way thither.

Instead of a general hope in God's mercies, (which those have little reason to rely upon, who despise the gracious offers of mercy tendered to them by the Gospel) we have the pardon of our sins sealed to us in the *blood* of the *new covenant*.

Instead

the HOLY SCRIPTURES. 285

Inſtead of the obſcure notices of a future ſtate which reaſon offers, we have *life and immortality brought to light* by him, who is the *firſt-born from the dead* [c], and the *firſt fruits of them that ſleep* [d] : who died that he might deſtroy death, and free us from the dominion of it [e], and roſe again to aſſure us of a life after death, and convince us that he had all power given him by God to beſtow eternal life upon as many as were duly qualified for it [f]. Our Saviour's viſible aſcenſion into heaven, was a lively and ſenſible inſtance of the rewards of another world: and it is matter of unſpeakable comfort to all good Chriſtians, to conſider that he is gone into heaven, as our *forerunner, to prepare a place for us* [g], in thoſe manſions of bliſs, where he ſits at God's right hand,

[c] Coloſ. i. 18. [d] 1 Cor. xv. 20. [e] Heb. ii. 14, 15. [f] John xvii. 2. Rom. xiv. 9. See 1 Cor. i. 21. [g] John xiv. 2. Heb. vi. 20.

and

and makes intercession for us, as a *merciful and faithful high-priest*, who is both able and willing to *succour them that are tempted* [h], being touched with a compassionate sense of the weaknesses and frailties of human nature; forasmuch *as in the days of his flesh* he himself was compassed about with the same infirmities, and was *in all points tempted like as we are* [i]. All which considerations give us all imaginable assurance, that if we be not wanting to ourselves, *nothing will be able to separate us from the love of God, in Jesus Christ our Lord.* [k].

The sacred writers never speak upon this subject, but in a triumphant stile, and in a holy rapture of spiritual joy. *It is Christ, that died*, saith St. *Paul* [l], *yea, rather that is risen again, who is even at the right hand*

---

[h] Heb. ii. 17, 18. [i] Συμπάθησον ἡμῖν ὅτι τὴν ἀσθενείαν τῆς σαρκὸς αὐτοπαθῶς ἐπείρασας. Clem. Alex. Pædagog. l. 1. c. 8. [k] Rom. viii. 39. [l] Ibid. v. 33, &c.

of God, *who makes intercession for us*; and in all our adversities *we shall be more than conquerors through him that loved us. When Christ who is our life shall appear, we shall appear with him in glory*, saith the same Apostle [h]. To the same purpose are those admirable words of St. *Peter* [i], *whom not seeing ye love, in whom, though now ye see him not, yet believing, ye rejoice with joy unspeakable and full of glory*. All which expressions so full of heavenly comfort are grounded upon the words of Christ himself, recorded by St. *John, because I live, ye shall live also* [k] : And again, at the beginning of the *Revelation*, [l] where our Saviour appearing to St. *John* supports and confirms his faith by those remarkable words, *fear not, I am the first and the last : I am he that liveth and was dead, and behold I am alive for ever-*

[h] Colos. iii. 3. [i] 1 Pet. i. 8. [k] John xiv. 19. [l] Chap. i. 17, 18.

more, and have the keys of hell and of death.

What arguments can reason suggest to us of God's love toward mankind, which are comparable to those that are taken from this consideration, that *he has given us his Son* * ? The greatest gift that he was able to bestow, or we capable of receiving. Or what motives of obedience can be so forcible, as those which our Saviour's wonderful love and kindness, his amazing humility and condescension do furnish us with? when we reflect upon all that he has done and suffered for us, the obligations he hath laid upon us, and the right that he has to our service, as having purchased us with the price of his blood. What a powerful persuasive to obedience do those words of Christ contain in them, *° As my Father has loved*

* John iii. 16.
° John xv. 9, 10.

me, so have I loved you; continue ye in my love: If ye keep my commandments, ye shall abide in my love. To reflect upon his love constraining us, gratitude obliging us, redemption engaging us to be his servants, does without question afford the strongest comforts against our fears, the greatest encouragement to the performance of our duty, and the most powerful preservative in the time of temptation, that can be desired.

And do these consolations of God seem small unto us? or is there any secret method of obtaining heaven and happiness, which hath been luckily found out by the *wits of the present age*, as much inferior to their *heathen predecessors* in parts, as they are in ingenuity, after it had lain hid so long, and was undiscovered by all the eminent sages of the *Gentile* world? Who miserably groped like the blind in their search after heavenly truth, and wish for a better guide than they found their own reason to be be ' to direct them in the untrodden paths of *pure and undefiled religion*.

So great is our natural blindness in things relating to God, so great is the averseness of our wills to the spiritual exercises of Religion, that all the helps both of nature and grace are little enough to enable us rightly to discharge our duty ᵐ. Surely then God's mercy ought to be thankfully acknowledged if he vouchsafes us greater measures of

---

ˡ Utinam tàm facile vera invenire possem, quàm falsa convincere: *Cic. lib.* 1. *de Nat. Deor.* There is a remarkable passage to the same Purpose in *Plato*'s Phædro, *cap.* 23. where speaking of the enquiries of reason, concerning a future state, he compares its assistance to a boat or vessel that carries us through the waves of this troublesome world, and then adds this further reflexion: Εἰ μή τις δύναιτο ἀσφαλέστερον καὶ ἀκινδυνότερον ἐπὶ βεβαιοτέρου ὀχήματος, ἢ ΘΕΙΟΥ ΛΟΓΟΥ τινὸς διαπορον θῆναι: unless a man can have a safer and securer passage by the help of some stronger vessel, or a Divine Revelation.

ᵐ Ecce adhuc tepescimus, auditis tot signis tuis & doctrinis: quid fieret, si tantum lumen ad te se quendum non haberemus? *Kempis de imit. Christi, lib.* 3. *c.* 18.

strength

strength and knowledge in order to this end, than the bare light and powers of nature can furnish us with: And it is a great argument both of his wisdom and goodness, that when *sin had so much abounded* in the world, *grace should much more abound.*

The Conclusion.

FOR a conclusion to the whole, I shall give the reader a general view of the reasons which prove the Scriptures to be the word of God; all which joined together will amount to the force of a demonstration.

In short then; this book contains the most ancient records which are extant in the world, and informs us of the most remarkable occurrences that ever happened in it. It gives us an account of the beginning of the world, and affords us a prospect unto the end of it: nay, it leads us beyond it, and shews us the way to a better, *that new heaven, and new earth, wherein dwells righteousness.*

These holy writings are the only means of coming to the knowledge of God and of ourselves: they open an intercourse between heaven and earth, by the account they give us of the several transactions between God and man, especially the wonderful contrivance of man's redemption, and that gracious covenant made with him by God in Christ.

The *Bible* instructs us in such sublime truths, as are sufficient to raise admiration in the greatest understandings, and yet delivers them in such plainness and simplicity of expression, as is proper at once to inform, and to affect the meanest capacities. It lays down the most perfect rules and directions for all states and conditions of life, offers the most powerful motives to persuade men to practise accordingly.

Although the several books of it were written in distant ages, by persons of different qualities, conditions and interests, with great variety both of matter and manner of expression; yet they all agree in teaching the same fundamental truths, and promoting one and the same excellent design, *viz.* the glory of God, and the eternal happiness of men. The several parts of holy Writ do likewise corroborate each other's testimony; what one part promises, the other performs; what is prophesied in the *Old Testament,* we find accomplished in the *New.*

Thus far the holy Scriptures carry their own evidence along with them. But if we proceed to examine the external proofs of their divine authority, we shall find ourselves encompassed with a whole *cloud of witnesses.*

These holy books have stood the test of the most inquisitive men in all ages, and bore up against the injuries of time itself, that devours all things, *Jews* and *Gentiles,* as well as *Christians,* have some way or other given testimony to their truth. The *heathens* never durst call in question the principal miracles therein related,

which

which are the credentials of its divine authority, and the *seal* which God hath set to this his *will and testament*. The oldest monuments of the heathen story, and all their ancient theology is derived from the Scriptures [k], though disguised with fables for the confirming their own superstitions and idolatries.

The *Jews* are zealous asserters of the authority of those very prophecies which bear witness to that Christ whom they themselves refuse to acknowledge.

The Christians of all ages, a great and venerable body of men, have reverenced these books as the oracles of heaven. No body ever thoroughly searched into them, and lived up to their directions, that ever found cause to repent them of their pains. On the contrary, the wisest and best

---

[k] *See this fully proved by the learned* Huetius, *in his* Quæstiones Alnetanæ, & Demonstrat. Evangel. *Prop.* 4. *cap.* 3. &c.

of men, the more they have studied them, the more cause they have found to admire them, and still the greater comfort and satisfaction they have felt, by being devoutly exercised in them.

To conclude, if this book every way answers all the ends of Revelation, if it proposes suitable remedies to all the defects of human nature, if it setteth forth natural truths in their proper light, and discovers supernatural ones in a way worthy of the majesty of God, and most effectual to give satisfaction to the inquisitive minds of men: I say, if all these characters of a divine original are to be found in these holy Writings, and in none other, then we must conclude, either that God never vouchsafed to make any extraordinary Revelation of his will to the world, or that the Scriptures which we embrace as the word of God are that very Revelation.

I shall

I shall close up this argument with those excellent words of *Tatian*, in his oration to the *Greeks*, where he gives this account of his conversion to Christianity [d] : *When I gave my mind,* faith he, *to a serious search after truth, it happened that I met with books written in a barbarous language, which, in respect to the doctrine contained in them, were much older than any writings of the* Greeks, *and contained divine truths in opposition to their errors and superstitions. And I was fully convinced of the truth of these writings, from the plainness and unaffectedness of the stile, from the sincerity of the writers, from the intelligible account they give of the creation*

---

[d] Περινοοῦντί μοι τὰ σπουδαῖα συνέβη γραφαῖς τισι βαρβαρικαῖς, πρεσβυτέραις, μὲν ὡς πρὸς τα Ἑλλήνων δόγματα, θειοτέραις δὲ ὡς πρὸς τὴν ἐκείνων πλάνην. Καί μοι πεισθῆναι ταύταις συνέβη, διά τι τῶν λέξεων τὸ ἄτυφον, καὶ τῶν εἰπόντων τὸ ἀπεριτήδευτον, καὶ τῆς τοῦ παντὸς ποιήσεως τὸ εὐκατάληπτον, καὶ τῶν μελλόντων τὸ προγνωστικὸν, καὶ τῶν παραγγελμάτων τὸ ἐξαίσιον, καὶ τῶν ὅλων τὸ μοναρχικόν. Tatian. Orat. ad Græcos, n. 46. Edit. Oxon.

of the world, from the prophetical foresight they contain of things to come, from the excellency of their precepts, and because the whole design of those books is to instruct men in the knowledge and worship of the one true God.

With what reverence and attention, with what joy and gladness ought we then to receive these holy oracles? *not as the words of men,* extreamly liable to error and uncertainty, especially in matters of the greatest importance, *but as they are in truth the words of God,* the author of eternal happiness, and the only infallible guide and conductor thither. When many withdraw themselves from our Saviour's instructions, St. *Peter* thus expressed his steady adherence to his Master's words and doctrine [1], *Lord,* saith he, *to whom should we go? thou hast the words of eternal life.* And we may justly ap-

[1] John vi. 68.

ply the fame words to our own cafe, to confirm ourfelves in our moſt holy faith; and when we find it attacked by the open aſſaults, or fly infinuations of our modern fceptics and infidels, this will be a fufficient reply to demand of them, *to whom ſhall we go?* Shall we go to the men of reafon? But every man is forward to think his own reafon as good as his neighbour's; and reafon never puts on fo many different fhapes, as when it undertakes to determine points of religion. Or fhall we apply ourfelves to the philofophers for greater certainty and better information? *the holy Writings alone contain the words of eternal life*; a truth which the wifeſt heathens never arrived to a certain knowledge of themfelves, much lefs could they give their fcholars any fatisfaction or aſſurance in fo important a point: *Learn of me*, faith our Saviour [b], *for I am meek and*

[b] Matth. xi. 29.

lowly of heart, and ye shall find rest unto your souls. Let us learn of him, the gentlest Master, and the kindest Instructor, who will have compassion on our ignorances, and help our infirmities, who will supply our imperfections with his own all-sufficient merits, and reward those good works which he himself hath wrought in us, with an *eternal weight of glory.* His laws are the light of our eyes, and the joy of our hearts; his Gospel is a *guide of the blind, an instructor of the foolish, a teacher of babes, a light that shines in a dark place,* and clears up the doubts of our dim reason; and if we follow, its conduct will lead thro' this vale of misery into those blessed regions, where there is light, and life, and happiness for evermore.

A short

A short Prayer to be used by any one alone in the Morning.

I Adore thee, O Lord, the possessor of Heaven and Earth : Who surpasseth all our thoughts, and dost us good beyond all our desires. There is all reason that I should acknowledge thee continually; that I should worship and praise, and love, and obey thee, whilst I have my Being. I cannot but witness against myself, whensoever I neglect thee; much more when I oppose thy most high authority, by doing contrary to thy laws. For thy almighty goodness gave me my Being; and by that alone have I been maintained and liberally provided for: Yea, it hath born with me very patiently in my rebellion, and used extraordinary means to make us Friends, and ceases not its intreaties after many unkind denials; but continues to importune me, me, till my heart consent to yield itself intirely to thee.

I cannot with-hold myself, O Lord, from thee, when I consider what thou art, and what thou hast been to me: Such a tender gracious and compassionate father, as my greatest affections cannot find words to express. I must again surrender soul and body into thy hands, which have been so long, so lovingly stretched out toward me: Resolving to stay with thee, and never to depart away from thee.

For the more I know of thee, the more I find that I must needs love thee: And the more I love thee, the more I desire to love thee, and to resemble thee, and to be beloved of thee. O that I may feel the power of thy love so great in my heart, that it may govern the rest of my passions and affections. And nothing in the World may tempt me to displease thee, but every thing provoke me more to love thee, and delight in thee, and obey thee, *For whom is there*

A Prayer for the Morning.

there in Heaven that I can desire but thee, or on earth besides thee! who art the blessed and only Potentate, the King of Kings, and Lord of Lords; who only hast immortality? And designest by thy Son Jesus to raise us, sinful Dust and Ashes, to a Kingdom, Glory, Honour and Immortality in the Heavens.

I most earnestly beseech thee that this sense of thee may accompany me wheresoever I go, and in whatsoever I do this day. That approving myself to thee in such a godly, sober, righteous, charitable and prudent behaviour, as may adorn the Gospel of my Lord and Master Christ Jesus; I may have a greater assurance of thy good will towards me, and an undoubted hope of thy mercy in him to eternal life. In whose most blessed name and words I humbly recommend myself, my friends, and all thy servants to thy infinite charity; saying, as he hath taught us,

Our Father, &c.

Another for the Evening.

BLessing, Glory, Honour, and Praise be again returned to thee, O father of mercy, from a most thankful heart; which offers up itself also in holy devotion to thee. Who art my sovereign Lord, my most loving Saviour, my deliverer and benefactor; the fountain of all the good things I enjoy at present, and the hope of my soul for ever and ever. Blessed be thy renewed kindness to me this day past: Both to myself and my relations, to my soul and my body, in my transactions with men, and in the liberty thou allowest me of addresses to thyself. Pardon, good Lord, whatsoever hath escaped me in thought, word, or deed, contrary to my duty: And accept of those sincere intentions, and unfeigned purposes, which were, and I hope shall always be in my heart to study to approve myself to thee in all well-doing.

It is but just and reasonable that I should follow thy Will, and not my own:

A Prayer for the Evening.

own: And in a grateful sense of what I have received from thee, I ought to be moved to employ all the powers of my Soul and Body for thee. But such is the Goodness of thy Will, that it is for my ease and pleasure, and greatest happiness to be absolutely led and governed by it. I am sensible, O Lord, how much I am indebted to thee for teaching me by Christ Jesus, and also strongly obliging me to exercise myself to all godliness, purity, righteousness, humility, goodness and truth. And accordingly I thank thee, above all things, for his holy instructions and example; for the hope thou hast given us by his blood, that thou wilt be so merciful to our sins, as not to deny us the power of thy Holy Spirit to enable us to follow him, and obey his commands; and for that exceeding great and precious promise which he hath given us of immortal life, to encourage us to follow him willingly and chearfully, even to the Death.

O that I may feel a lively and stedfast faith in his word, continually
working

working with great power in my heart, exciting me to an unwearied diligence, and zeal, and love, and patient continuance in my duty towards thee, and towards all Men: That so my hope in thee may grow and increase, and I may joyfully expect that hour which shall translate me hence to the eternal happiness of the other World. And during my stay here, I commend myself to thy good providence, which hath hitherto been so tender of me. I trust thee wholly with myself, and all belonging to me: And am willing in every thing to be disposed of, as thou seest good. This night I flee unto thy almighty protection; hoping thou wilt keep me safely, and whether I wake in this or the other life, I shall still be praising thee; whose mercy endureth for ever, *Amen*; for Christ Jesus his sake, by whom thou hast encouraged me to hope in thee, and taught me to call thee father; saying,

Our Father, &c.

THE TABLE.

A Synopsis   Page 11
The Introduction   27

CHAP. I.

That the several Parts of Scripture were accommodated to Mens Use, with a regard to their several Capacities; which appears by the different Subjects therein treated of, and the different Stiles wherein the several Parts of Scripture are written   33
The Reason of the different Stiles used in the several Parts of Holy Writ   36
The use that unlearned Persons should make of this difference   39

CHAP. II.

Two Prejudices which hinder many from the careful reading and Study of the Scriptures, the first of them, relating to the Stile and Method of those holy Writings, considered   42
The peculiar Advantages of receiving Instruction from the Scriptures themselves   44
A defence of the Scripture Stile comprized in four Particulars.
1. As to the Historical Books, the principal matters are there recorded with such Circumstances as mutually confirm and support each other   45

2. The

The TABLE.

2. The harmony and agreement between the old and new Teſtament is a convincing proof of the truth of both 48
3. It was fit that the myſtery of our redemption ſhould be opened by degrees, according to the capacities and exigencies of ſeveral ages 51
4. The plain and inartificial Stile which the holy Writers make uſe of, is a great Argument of their Truth and Sincerity 55
A ſhort defence of ſuch Paſſages as ſeem to contain trivial and inconſiderable Matters 60

CHAP. III.

An anſwer to another popular Objection againſt the reading of the Scriptures, taken from their obſcurity: and ſome Rules laid down to remedy this Difficulty 62
All things neceſſary to ſalvation are plainly revealed 63
General Reaſons aſſigned of the obſcurity of the Scriptures 67
From hence appears the Obligation lying upon the unlearned to ſubmit to the judgment of their lawful Paſtors 71
Four Rules laid down for the right underſtanding of the Scriptures.

I. Rule, that we ſhould begin with reading the plaineſt Books 76
II. Rule, that we ſhould have a regard to the analogy of Faith in judging of the ſenſe of particular Texts 78

III. Rule,

The TABLE.

III. Rule, to compare one place of Scripture with another 82
IV. Rule, to have an especial regard to the judgment and practice of the primitive Church 86

This Rule of great use to silence the disputes about Church-Government 91
The inference from the whole, that we ought to read the Scriptures with humility and reverence 95

CHAP. IV.

Concerning the historical Books of the old Testament, and what things are chiefly observable in our reading of them 96
A general division of the Books of the old Testament, into Historical, Moral, the Psalms and the Prophets 97
The advantages of the Scripture history above all other histories 99
Several passages in the three first chapters of Genesis explained and vindicated from the exceptions in the Theoria Sacra, and Archæologia 100
Two schemes or Systems of Religion, laid down in the writings of Moses 104
Reasons assigned for the ritual ordinances in the law of Moses. 108
Concerning the account Moses gives of God's chusing Abraham's family, and the promise of the Messias 129

The TABLE.

The old Testament *history an evident proof of an over-ruling providence* 130
The Scripture *history of the Jewish nation writ with greater care and fidelity than those of other countries.* 133

CHAP. V.

Concerning the moral *writings of the* old Testament 137
The *usefulness of the* Book of Job 138
- - - - *And of the* Proverbs ; *and in what respects that book exceeds the writings of the heathen moralists* 139
The *proper use of* Ecclesiastes 143

CHAP. VI.

Concerning the book of Psalms, *and their usefulness* 147
Two *objections against the use of them briefly considered* 153, 154

CHAP. VII.

Concerning the prophetical *writings, and their usefulness* 158
The *historical and prophetical books do mutually support and confirm each other* 159
The *uses we ought to make of the plain prophecies* 162
- - - - *And of the obscure ones* 165
The *several* Prophecies *have a mystical sense, proved* 169

The TABLE.

The reasons assigned why a mystical sense is sometimes involved under a literal   170

CHAP. VIII.

Observations upon the Gospels, *in order to the more useful reading that part of holy Scripture*   186
The difference between the new Covenant and the old   187
In the Gospels four things chiefly to be observed.

1. Our Saviour's doctrine, *which is delivered either in sermon or parables*   194
2. His miracles   210
The difference between true and false miracles briefly stated   ibid.
3. Our Lord's manner of life and conversation   214
4. The circumstances of his death   218

The marks of integrity which appear in the evangelical writings   222

CHAP. IX.

The principal matters to be observed in reading the Acts and Epistles of the Apostles   226
The success of the Apostles preaching an evident proof of the truth of Christianity   227
The several parts of the new Testament *do mutually confirm and support each other*   230

The TABLE.

The usefulness of the Acts and Epistles considered in three particulars.

1. As they are an authentic commentary upon the Gospels   234
2. As they give us an exact idea of the faith and manners of the first Christians   246
3. — — — And likewise of the graces and virtues of the Apostles themselves   253

A brief survey of the writings of St. Peter, St. James, and St. John   265

CHAP. X.

The advantages of Revelation above natural light, or any system of the law of nature   270

This proved by three arguments.

1. Because Revelation explains our duty more fully and distinctly   272
2. It enforces it by a more commanding authority   279
3. The arguments it makes use of are more powerful, and withal better suited to common capacities   282

The Conclusion   292

www.ingramcontent.com/pod-product-compliance
Lightning Source LLC
Chambersburg PA
CBHW031903220426
43663CB00006B/749